NINE DAYAK NIGHTS

Raseh, the co-author. He is the
leading spirit-medium of Mentu Tapu

NINE DAYAK NIGHTS

W. R. GEDDES

SINGAPORE
OXFORD UNIVERSITY PRESS
OXFORD NEW YORK

Oxford University Press

Oxford New York Toronto
Delhi Bombay Calcutta Madras Karachi
Petaling Jaya Singapore Hong Kong Tokyo
Nairobi Dar es Salaam Cape Town
Melbourne Auckland
and associated companies in
Berlin Ibadan

Oxford is a trade mark of Oxford University Press

© Oxford University Press 1957

First published 1957
Reissued as an Oxford University Press paperback 1985
Third impression 1991

ISBN 0 19 582621 3

Printed in Malaysia by Peter Chong Printers Sdn. Bhd.
Published by Oxford University Press Pte. Ltd.,
Unit 221, Ubi Avenue 4, Singapore 1440

CONTENTS

LIST OF PLATES

To
MAUD

my wife, who, in Mentu
Tapuh and elsewhere,
helped me so much

INTRODUCTION

ONE day in Sarawak, when I was doing anthropological field-work amongst the Land Dayaks, a villager told me that, for ten dollars, he would tell me a very good story. To a Britisher ten Sarawak dollars mean £1 3s 4d, and British anthropologists have always to operate on a budget of thrift. It was not, however, the amount which made me decline his kindness. True, it was formidable for one piece of information, but it was not yet beyond me. My concern was not so much about the price itself as about a precedent—or rather, and worse, about a principle with retrospective implications.

The date was early in November 1950. I had arrived in Sarawak in February 1949 to make a socio-economic study of the Land Dayaks, sponsored by the Colonial Social Science Research Council of the Colonial Office. The main purpose of such a study is to describe the arrangements under which a people gain their living, and the standard of it, in such a way as to show the relationships between these arrangements and the rest of their culture. A culture means what a people habitually do, think and feel, and the way in which the doing, thinking and feeling of any one of them depends on that of the others. There is only one way in which it can properly be studied: that is to live with the people, and to stay with them long enough to see all the main variations of their lives. A broad survey may be made first to find the most suitable group for close study, and general conclusions may be checked in other groups, but one community the anthropologist must know intimately. The community I chose was the village of Mentu Tapuh. For five months in 1950 my wife joined me, and it is to her that I owe the friendly relationship which I established with the most important part of the community—the children.

To reach this village one went by jeep from Kuching, the capital of Sarawak, for forty miles to the end of the Colony's longest road—to use a polite term for it as it then was—and thence by canoe up the serpentine Kedup tributary of the Sadong river. The distance of this canoe journey to Mentu Tapuh, lying about an hour's walk away from Indonesian Borneo, was probably not more than forty or fifty miles,

but the time it would take could never be predicted. During the
monsoon a lucky thunderstorm might bring just the right fresh to the
stream. Then an outboard motor could be used on the canoe and,
if all went well, the distance could be covered in seven hours. But a
fresh was a hindrance if it were too high, for then at times the canoe
was ensnared between the tops of trees meeting from opposite banks.
The situation was very different during the drier months. Then the
stream, blocked by great dams formed by fallen tree-trunks with
smaller drift-wood piling behind them, and with countless fantastic
snags sticking up from its many shallows, looked to a weary traveller
like the Styx. At such times the journey up to the village could never
be done in under two days. The stream soon acquainted the stranger
with the closer meaning of natural forces to the people who lived
in the villages dotted every ten miles or so along its forested or grass-
tangled banks.

Not that the varying moods of the stream affected me in the same
way, or to anything like the same extent, as they did the people themselves. Not blessed with outboard engines, they vastly preferred the
journey on the Styx to the journey on the flood. The stream had an
enduring place in their lives, connecting them to the outside world.
Up it, fairly often, came Chinese or Malay traders, and sometimes the
District Officer on a quick tour. Down it the men, and more rarely the
women, went, perhaps for most once or twice a year, on visits to the
bazaar at Serian, where the road from Kuching ended. Down it, too,
if they wanted medical aid from the Government Dresser at Serian,
the people had to carry their sick, and then carry them home again
upstream. For them the journey was always long—four days on the
average, and at worst at least a week. There was a track also, but it
was devious, muddy and long, and in any case the sick could not
walk. Therefore the villagers lived and died for the most part in their
own community, with few visitors, and without the aid of modern
medicine.

Their lack in this respect was my greatest asset. A European anthropologist coming into a Dayak community enjoys many advantages
over his hosts, making him acceptable. Some of these it behoves him
to shake off as quickly as possible. One is the aura of power which
clings about him as a member of the governing race. Not that the
Land Dayaks resent European authority. They hold it in the highest
regard. Memories of the bad old head-hunting days remain vivid
enough to keep the people grateful for the peace which the White

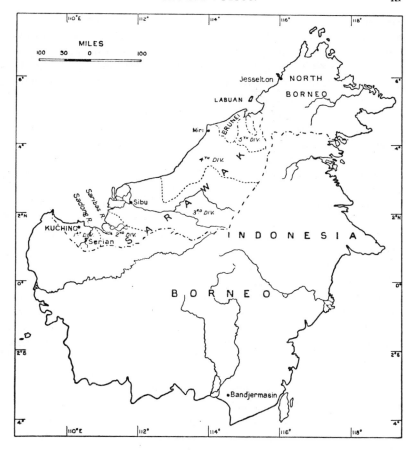

Rajah brought, for they were usually the hunted. Many of the heads which decorate Sea Dayak verandahs must be those of Land Dayaks, lost along with their land. The respect of Land Dayaks for European authority is, however, abstract. They dislike becoming the subjects of it, for, although they never quarrel with authority, they have in reality as stubborn a love of self-determination as any people on earth. They will not therefore easily relax in the fullness of their virtues and vice before anyone who they think may have come to boss. Other advantages, however, the anthropologist may exploit to the gain of both parties.

These advantages are several. In himself he is a fascination, from the first startling occasion on which he blows his nose with a snort to the clothes he wears or the way he eats his food. He is rich, and can give presents—to a man, perhaps, a shot-gun cartridge, to a girl fifty-cent jewellery or lipstick, to the children biscuits with blobs of icing on top—small to him but great to them. He has rare possessions, which delight: a gramophone; magazines—so fond were the little girls in illiterate Mentu Tapuh of the illustrated advertisements that they would sometimes kiss the faces of models displaying the latest West-end fashions, and the pages had to be rationed out amongst them; a camera giving them copies of their own pictures; a motor-driven boat in which some might ride without the labour of paddling. If the European is careful not to allow his possessions to be a barrier between himself and the people, he is helped by the trappings of his culture which inevitably he trails along with him.

With such advantages as these it did not matter to me that the Dayaks failed to appreciate dutiful explanations of anthropology, that they laughed at the claim that the outside world wished to know of their ways—they being, so they said, a people living dirtily in the jungle. It did not matter that a number of them secretly believed that my talk about their customs was hocus-pocus to cover a search for diamonds. Nobody minded a diamond-seeker, provided he found no diamonds—and unhappily I found none—so long as he was a beneficent and interesting seeker.

But, as time went on, one advantage outrivalled all the others. The Director of Medical Services for Sarawak most generously allowed me to draw from his store at Kuching whatever medical supplies my scant medical knowledge made me feel competent to use. How this generosity progressively helped my relationship with the people of Mentu Tapuh can be understood only in the light of their theory of disease and their methods of treating it.

It was generally believed that much of the serious sickness was caused by evil demons, who either wounded the patient internally, stayed in his body to work harm, or stole one of his seven souls which, combined, sustain his life. The treatment was generally to propitiate the demon with festivities, to use ritual to heal the wound or remove the sickness, and to recover the soul. Treatment could be had from three different classes of practitioner. The priests of the ancestral cult simply made offerings to the ancestors and to the demons, appealing to the demons to stop troubling the patient and to the ancestors to use their influence in seeing that they did. The priestesses of the women's

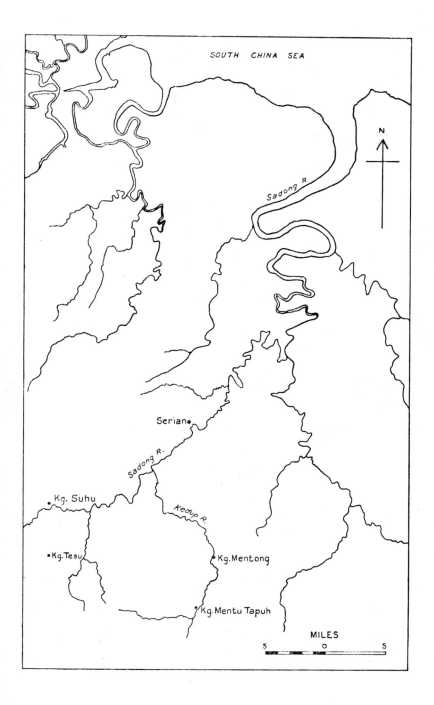

cult appealed in the same way to their own set of deities and to the demons, but went one stage further in actually catching the patient's lost soul, usually in the form of a small stone snatched out of the air, and returning it to him. Finally, there were in Mentu Tapuh two persons termed *manangs*.

The performances of the *manangs* were much more lively, making up in melodrama for their poorer sanction in tradition. These two practitioners diagnosed, prognosed, invoked deities, danced in semi-trance consulting their deities in person, derived power from special objects in their possession, demonstrated superhuman qualities, and caught souls. But the most important way in which they differed in their practice from the others was that they actually treated the patient, either by sucking or pulling the sickness out of him, or by using mysterious medicines, or both. There were other people in the village who gave herbal medicines, but only these practitioners did so as part of a spiritual treatment. The leading *manang*—or spirit-medium, or shaman, or medicine-man, or witch-doctor, for he was all of these—was a man about twenty-eight years old named Raseh.

The Land Dayak theory of disease was not naive. The people recognized the difference between proximate and remote causes, and if they could see, or thought they could see, an obvious cause for a complaint they did not look behind it for a more distant cause, except perhaps now and then in a theoretical way. Thus they would not let a man who had fallen down and broken his nose bleed while they searched for the demon who may have pushed him. It was much the same with certain common illnesses, such as malaria, which was often believed to be due to eating too much sugar-cane. For all complaints in this 'natural' category the people were from the very first keen to have such treatment as I was able to give. They already knew something of the value of European medicine, for some of them had visited the Government Dresser at Serian and others had been tended by the kind Catholic missionaries who sometimes visited the village.

Even when the obscurer complaints were assigned to an injury inflicted by a demon or to the activity of a demon working inside the patient, this did not reveal a primitive simplicity of mind. There is not a great deal of difference between a demon and a germ. Had the Dayaks been shown their too familiar germs through a microscope they would instantly have claimed confirmation of their theory. A known characteristic of demons is that they can make themselves minute at will. The nature of the agency, whether it was germ or

demon, mattered only insofar as it determined the means by which
it could be countered. Here the Dayaks diverged from rationalism
in believing that supernatural means provided one method, and in
many cases the best method. But they also believed that success might
attend a direct attack by medicines to drive out the demon or to
heal the internal wound. Thus they were not opposed to medicine
in itself. But they were strongly opposed to having it as the only
method by which they could treat their sick. Therefore to laugh at
their theory of disease, and to call their spiritualistic treatments silly,
was the very worst way of encouraging them to seek modern treatment.

It would also have been rather cruel. The ceremonies for the actually
sick, together with the larger festivals to keep sickness away from the
village, provided the highlights of the people's lives. So much of their
drama, dancing, singing and feasting depended upon them. Too sweeping
an attack on their theory of disease might do more than chase away the
mythical spirits of sickness. It could damage the spirits of the people
themselves. The Land Dayaks are very unlucky in having as the
support of so much of their aesthetic and recreational life a specific
supernatural belief. Such a simple, concrete belief is so much more
susceptible to rational attack than the beliefs of the universalistic
religions which, influenced more gradually by the impact of a slowly
growing freedom of thought and science, have been able to develop
the resilience of abstruse generalizations, hydra-headed in their
particular interpretations. A thorough attack on the Land Dayak
theory of disease, especially if extended to crop diseases, could ruin
their religion, and with it would go much of their present ceremony
and fun. The apostles of Christianity feel justified in making such an
attack. We shall pass over the fact that they strike their first blows with
the weapons of rationalism. We can only hope that they will carry
their attack through, giving the people new joys and new art to make
up for what they will have lost. A humble anthropologist had better
meddle less deeply.

Not because I thought the matter out clearly but by circumstance,
I followed a milder way, although I was nothing but dilatory in doing
so. When I thought someone might be helped by medicine I suggested
that he take it just in case it might do him some good. If he were
receiving spiritual treatment as well, and he recovered, he invariably
gave the credit to the spiritual treatment. Subconsciously, he may
have had different thoughts, induced partly no doubt by the trouble

and cost in food of a sickness ceremony. Gradually more and more people began to regard the medicine as the first rather than the second string to their bow. The result was that more forms of sickness, notably the dysentery of infants which previously caused more deaths than anything else, began to pass into the 'natural' category. This was a happy result. There were more than enough other cases, chronic or hopeless, as well as the prophylactic festivals, to provide plenty of ceremonies for the satisfaction of all those not absolutely *in extremis*.

In not every instance, however, could the European treatment be interlaced so harmoniously with that of the Dayak practitioners. A characteristic of their method was to impose a period of seclusion, usually seven days, upon the patient. During this period he should not leave his house. For treatment in the village this rule did not, of course, matter, but it did prevent a patient's going, or being taken, to the Government Dresser at Serian. Not only could this capable Chinese Dresser give the sick far better aid than I could, but he was also able to arrange for bad cases to be transported to the hospital at Kuching. With my power-driven boat I could take some sick persons with me when I visited Serian. The restriction rule did not normally trouble me. In the first place, the leading priest of the ancestral cult, who was also the headman of the village, was always ready to allow the rule to be broken if I suggested taking one of his patients. Secondly, there were always too many passengers for the boat, so that if a person preferred to remain behind, it could be, as far as I was concerned, his funeral. On one occasion, however, the rule brought me right into conflict with Raseh.

Raseh, the medicine-man, was a recalcitrant subject for an anthropologist—quite the worst in the village. He refused to play the game, being secretive. He would say in answer to pestering that he was to hold a ceremony at a particular time and place. Then he would hold it earlier, or in another place, excusing himself always plausibly. This secretiveness was not unwise. His performance, unlike those of the ancestral cult which depended upon invocations of a set form, needed the creation of a sense of mystic power. To this end he used a lot of trickery. With the best will in the world a stranger from another culture could not help but see through some of it, as when he proved his invulnerability by stamping upon upturned knife-blades which were placed in such a way, unperceived by the onlookers, that he could, through great skill and confidence, turn them flat without breaking his skin. His claims were fantastic and I think he believed in them as might an actor in a fantasy, intriguing an audience whose faith was complete. But he feared to be discredited. Therefore he was modest about displaying his talents before sceptical alien eyes. It was a pity, for his dancing, a principal feature of his ceremonies, far excelled that of any other villager.

While this game of hide-and-seek was still going on, a young man named Laduh fell ill. I thought he had appendicitis. He thought he had been cut inside by a demon. He thought this had happened because he had crossed over branches lying across the track into his paddy field.[1] To lay an obstacle across a person's track is believed to be a way of bringing the demons down upon him. We cannot here go into the question as to who had laid the branches there, and as to whether he had done so by accident or design, because it is a big question, which led to much talk, accusing and denying, in the village. But in case one may think that the Land Dayaks walk about burdened by superstitious dread, let it be said that had Laduh not in fact fallen sick he would probably never have thought again about the branches after he had kicked them aside. He was not so lucky, however. Therefore he thought he had been struck by a demon. His family thought so too. So did the village headman. So did all the villagers. And Raseh was quite sure. Raseh carried out a ceremony to heal the wound, and according to the rule, a seven-day restriction fell upon Laduh.

Laduh's illness concerned me. I had made a selection of persons of different ages and sex with a view to keeping an exact daily record of their activities and their diet for a whole year. Several months of the year had already passed, and Laduh had been the person chosen as the sample of the young unmarried men. By dying, he would have upset the plan. Furthermore, partly through our nightly conversations about his daily doings and partly for other indefinable reasons, he had come to be much more than a mere informant. At this time I was about to visit Kuching. I was keen to take Laduh with me, at least to Serian, and then on to Kuching if the Dresser decided he needed an operation.

I first found out about the seven-day restriction when I went to ask Laduh to come with me. It put me in a quandary. A good anthropologist should not change the course of events he has come to observe. But the course of events was likely to cause me trouble anyway. There was another circumstance which could be taken into account. Raseh was not regarded with unmixed respect in the village. Although

---

[1] *Paddy* is the term used for the plant which produces rice and also for the grain from this plant before it is husked.

his cult was favoured by many who liked a little melodrama mixed with their medicine and although it was accepted as one which had been practised at various times in the past, it did not have the essential role in village life that belonged to the ancestral cult. Had Raseh and his fellow *manang* stopped practising no one else would necessarily have taken their place. Considering these points, I concluded that I might fairly suggest to Laduh that he come with me despite the restriction. Once I did so, trouble came, and mounted.

The village headman, who was also the leading priest of the ancestral cult, had come along with me. He told Laduh that it would be dangerous for him to break the restriction, but that he could make up his own mind. After painful uncertainty, Laduh decided to take the risk. His ancient grandmother was incensed, and vigorously changed his mind back for him. I was rather sorry I had intervened, but felt a need now to persist. My arguments had, of course, shaken Laduh's faith in the value of the treatment he was getting from Raseh, so that his chances of recovery had become much less if he did stay at home. But further talk only made matters worse. Laduh became fully persuaded that he should break the restriction. But his grandmother had used a forceful argument. He now passed it on to me. 'Grandfather,' he said—a term which could be extended to any elderly man in the village and was applied to me as a courtesy, although hardly as a compliment, 'I should like to come with you. I feel I may die here otherwise. But you know what happens when a restriction is broken. I may get well myself, but anyone else in my household may be hurt in return. My infant brother over there may die.'

We left Laduh behind. He said he would come with me the next time I went to Serian, when the restriction would be over. He was lucky not to die, because he did have appendicitis.

Laduh was better when we returned. Just before I was due to go to Kuching again, he suffered another, worse attack. This time a ceremony was carried out by the leading priest of the ancestral cult, and a further restriction came to keep Laduh at home. The priest agreed to waive it. It was right against the rules of his religion that he should do so, but he was a man who thought it ridiculous that a Rajah—for so he called himself, with a twinkle in his eye—should have to obey the law of which he was the head. The grandmother was outraged. But Laduh went to Kuching, induced by a reminder of his earlier promise. I left him in hospital when I returned to the village.

Only a few days after our return, Raseh came to see me. His wife was ill. She was not menstruating, although she was not pregnant. He was worried about her. Would I take her to the hospital at Kuching? I told him to treat her himself. He said he could not do so because her sickness was not caused supernaturally. What could be said to such an answer! Raseh may have been ingenuous, but I thought him to be ingenious, and believed that I could see the workings of his mind. He restricted his practice to complaints which he thought he could cure. By these cases he proved his ability as a therapist. Cases he thought he could not cure he declared outside his scope, so they did not undermine faith in him. It might be said that any medical specialist behaves in the same way. But there was in fact a great difference, or so we hope, between the man in Harley Street and Raseh in Mentu Tapuh. The difference lay in the role of diagnosis. Each may have specialized in a single class of complaint, but whereas, scrupulously, the Harley Street man would confine his treatments to the complaints which fell into that class, Raseh, scrupulously too, would bring all treatable complaints into the class. Perhaps the difference has not been expressed very clearly. It is rather a subtle point of medical theory. In short, it may be said that Raseh was the less rigid diagnostician, the more expansive in his approach, the less hide-bound.

He should have been the more consistently successful too, but in fact his patients often responded poorly, and sometimes they even died. It may have been that my insight into his mind was false, or it may have been—as I think most likely—that his pure love of medicine, amounting in this case to stagecraft, made it hard for him to refuse a case. At any rate he had his failures. These he had to excuse with a variety of explanations, the most usual being that he had been consulted too late—another link with Harley Street.

Once set on this line of thought I did realize that Raseh was professionally correct in wishing to have his wife treated by a colleague rather than by himself. We debated the issue, and in the course of the debate an unspoken compact arose that in future we would open our medical cupboards to each other. When I next went to Kuching I took Raseh's wife to the hospital. Although she never fully regained her health, Raseh was grateful—more so than other persons and far more so than the lightness of the service warranted. From this time on he not only told me exactly when and where he was holding his ceremonies but did his best to arrange them at the most convenient times. We also had a most friendly relationship otherwise.

It was because we had this friendly relationship, that I was rather

hurt when Raseh placed a price of ten dollars upon the long story which
he offered to tell me. This was the first time I had ever been asked for
money in return for information. Most of it had come in the give-
and-take of talk on topics of interest, and the rest had been given out
of good will. Raseh's suggestion seemed alien to this atmosphere of
informality, as though I were a stranger who should go to a village
bargain counter. Furthermore, if I paid him, why should I not pay
all the others, particularly the leading priest of the ancestral cult who
had gone to many hours of trouble, and some spiritual risk, to give the
complete semi-secret prayers of his cult? The economy of the village
had very little cash in it, and I was quite content to keep it that way.
As I did not charge Raseh for anything I did for him, he should not
charge for anything he did for me. So I told him.

As usually happened in my differences of opinion with the villagers,
Raseh was right and I was wrong. He was offering to undertake a
specific task which he would not normally do and which certainly
could not be done through the pleasantries of conversation or in an
idle hour. If a Land Dayak does special work for anyone else, he
expects payment, either in return labour, in paddy, or in money.
Raseh knew that he would not get labour from me, and he knew
that I had no paddy. Therefore he expected money. The value in the
village of a day's labour was one dollar or its equivalent, but sometimes persons could get more by working as boatmen for Chinese
rubber traders. Of course, it did not occur to me when Raseh referred to his story as long that it was so long—not quite as long as
he, a financial optimist, reckoned, but far longer than I imagined.
Thus I thought the price too high, and told him that I could not
promise him any money at all. Raseh did not mind that the matter
was considered on a mercenary plane—after all, he had put it there—
but he was hurt at his story's being valued poorly. His story meant
much more to him than money, and *ars gratia artis* he dearly wanted
to tell it.

★   ★   ★

Not only did I fail to realize the length of the story but I mistook
its nature. Land Dayak stories may be divided into several classes
according to their main effect. Apart from purely historical legends,
which are few and sketchy, because the people prefer their present
to their unhappy and disturbed past, the stories forming the most
important class are those which account for the origin of practices

peculiar to the culture, particularly religious ritual. We could call these stories validatory myths. They are not referred to very much. Many villagers may not even have heard some of them. But they give the practices a rationale with which to face curious persons who may call them in question. They prove that the practices are customs, sanctioned long ago, by beings who were more than ordinary mortals.

One story in this class is that about Sibaok. It validates features of the graded festivals of the ancestral cult. It begins with an incident rather like one of those in the story Raseh wished to tell. Sibaok was a boy who lived long ago. One day he climbed up a coconut palm growing near his parents' home in the longhouse to get some coconuts to drink. When he reached the top of the palm, he saw that what he had thought was the sky was in fact a fruit-tree of the *sibu* species, much like the cultivated *rambutan* tree of the Malays. It was growing the opposite way to the coconut palm, so that as Sibaok continued his climb from the palm on to it he made his way down its trunk. When he reached the bottom he was in the land of the sky. He went across the sky until he came to the moon. To understand the manner in which he was received by the moon we must turn to another story telling who the moon was.

At one time upon the earth there was a man called Kaleng Buran. Normally he was of shining beauty, but once a month worms would break out all over his body making him a loathsome sight. In order to hide this disease from his lovely wife, he would retire to the temporary hut in his paddy field whenever an attack was near. Spying upon him there one day, his wife saw him in his diseased state. She returned immediately to the village in disgust. When Kaleng Buran himself came back to the village after his attack was over, his wife inside their house had barred the door against him. Time after time he begged his wife to let him in, but she, not knowing that he was once more glowingly handsome, would not answer. At last, in desperation, shame and spite, he called out to his wife that he was leaving for the sky, and carried out his threat by going up there to become the moon. His wife, in love with his brightness, lived on to become the nightjar, for ever uttering her call on moonlit nights.[1]

Sibaok wished to stay with the moon, but the moon told him of the complaint to which he was prone once a month. He said that at that time he smelt badly, so that Sibaok would find his company

[1] For a fuller account of the story of Kaleng Buran, see Nyandoh, *Sarawak Museum Journal*, vol. 5, No. 3, p. 415.

nauseating. Sibaok therefore continued his journey across the sky until he came to the Pleiades. The stars in this constellation were in fact seven brothers, whom, on account of their age, Sibaok addressed by the term 'grandfather'.

The seven brothers gave him a series of tasks to do. Here the details of the story become dull to non-Dayaks not familiar with the particular symbols used at ceremonies, and we shall not give them. It is enough to say that in the nature of the tasks lay the charter[1] for the use of many of the objects featured in Dayak festivals. For example, the stars told Sibaok to go to inspect their pig-traps. When he reached the place where he had been told the traps were set, he found instead a clump of bamboo of the *buruh* variety. He shook it, and wild pigs fell from the bamboo. Therefore, at the largest festivals, the grade of which is symbolized by the use of pigs as offerings, this species of bamboo must be used to make the offering platforms and to provide some of the decorations.

We can leave Sibaok at this stage of his adventure. He did, of course, eventually get down to earth again, collecting a lot of useful information *en route*, and landing right on top of the roof of his house to surprise his parents in the middle of their mourning. Knowledge of myths of this class makes the understanding of ceremonial simpler to the observer, accounting for its details and explaining their relative importance. In some cases it may do more. It may give him an idea of ceremonial which he has not been able to see. The myths are more than validations. They are also to some extent mnemonics.

For many years there had been no ceremony in Mentu Tapuh for the reception of heads, because of the drying-up of the supply owing to the Government's disapproval of head-hunting. I wanted to know what the ceremony was like, and why it was held. After all, an anthropologist from Borneo would be accounted a disappointing fellow indeed if he could say nothing on the subject of head-hunting. Only cannibalism attracts Europeans more. It did not occur to me that there might be a myth giving validating details of the festival held when heads were brought home to the village. And it did not occur to the people to tell me if there was, for they were not anthropologists.

Closely related in type to the myths which validate religious ritual are those which explain outstanding, strange, or especially meaningful

[1] The term used by Malinowski. See B. Malinowski, *Myth in Primitive Psychology* (London, 1926), p. 38.

features of the environment, or which account for the ups-and-downs of human fortune. Their common effect is to make the world less perturbing, either by taking the puzzle out of things or by taking the fortuity out of fate. They give a form to the world, painting it in excitingly and often amusingly.

The story of the origin of the moon could be put into this second class. Also into it could go an incident which occurs in the myth of Sibaok. The Pleiades give him as his first task the construction of a new outer verandah for their longhouse. Sibaok makes it in the usual Dayak fashion with many piles to keep it steady. The Pleiades disapprove. They tell him that he must have only a single pile in the centre, so that the verandah may tilt towards any of its corners. In different years, they say, it may take on different tilts, and the part of the earth below to which it is tilted in any year will that year have the best paddy harvests. The Dayak farmer whose paddy does poorly can thus take consolation in the thought that the Pleiades will favour him in due course. He knows that the constellation plays a role in his affairs, for its dawn rising marks the time when he must begin to clear fields for the new season and the beginning of its decline marks the time when he must plant his seed.

One more story in this class should be given, because it leads us to an important mode of Land Dayak thought different from the peculiar mode which we regard as proper for mankind. The story accounts for the presence in the stream a short distance above Mentu Tapuh of an ancient hardwood log, which is regarded as a village talisman and is given offerings at the times of the largest festivals. It is said that once upon a time in Java a man called Baji became angry with the sun, because it had killed his mother by its heat as she was working in her paddy field. He decided to kill the sun. To reach it, he cut down a *tantang* tree to use as a step-way. When he reached the top of it, he joined on a further tree to provide more steps, and so on, until he came close to the sun. For his very last series of steps he added the hardwood log. But while he had been climbing higher and higher, the white ants had been busy chewing away the base of the *tantang* tree. Just as he finished tying on the hardwood log, his whole step-way collapsed. Baji himself was killed. The hardwood log landed in its present place near Mentu Tapuh. Several generations ago a leading man of the village met in a dream the supreme deity who told him that the log had been the step of Baji, and that it should be venerated as a talisman by the villagers.

Now surely it is strange that a log, no matter how remarkable, should be regarded as having supernatural power? To the Dayaks it is highly unusual but it is not strange, for it is consistent with a principle of their thought—a principle often misunderstood as entirely religious whereas it is really logical. Let us spend a moment or two explaining it. If we stray for this little time in the swamp of philosophy, it is only that we may learn something about the mental countryside in which faith in the log is set.

The Dayaks believe, some clearly and some obscurely, that every object, but particularly those growing or usable or capable of changing in any way, has in it a kind of force. It must have, they say, for otherwise it could not grow or be used or change. We could translate their term for this force as 'soul', since it is the same term they use for the vital force in themselves, but if we do we may be trapped by the narrowness of our own concept into the foolishness of thinking that the Dayaks do not know the difference between human beings and other things. The truth of the matter is that the Dayaks tend to take a different view from us of cause and effect. Effects just do not follow passively from causes but must have in them a power in order to be able to develop. A spear can fly through the air in a way that a feather cannot because it has a different power. The force which we so nearly translated as 'soul' is thus the operative power in things.

Is not this Dayak view a childlike, personalistic one, due to their thinking that because they have a force when they do something everything must have a force enabling it to do something? It is personalistic, certainly. But is not our own view personalistic also, and especially childlike in its pride? We conclude that because we can produce consequences, all consequences follow passively from active agents like ourselves, which we term causes, amongst which we generally think of ourselves as alone autonomous, unless we are old-fashioned enough to acknowledge a God, remarkably like ourselves.

The fact is that for us common men—as distinct from the erudite philosophers—there are two possible metaphysical views of the world and our place in it, both of them faulty. The one is autocratic and the other is democratic. Neither is much good as a final explanation of sequences, and both have their problems and dangers. The danger of our autocratic view is the quite special place it gives to the human will, which is no doubt why we are shocked at the thought of a mechanical man and why we can allow only a single God, Himself difficult to account for. The chief problem left by our view is how to explain such things as the way great oaks from little acorns grow.

The Dayaks, on the other hand, with their more democratic grant of force to everything, do not share these concerns. Although they might be frightened by a mechanical man, they would not have their philosophy shattered by his arrival. If they had great oaks, instead of greater honey-trees, in their jungle, they could quite well understand their growing from little acorns. Indeed it may be because they have to deal so much with living things and we with manufactured things that each of our societies has a bias in favour of a different mode of thought out of the two open to us. Finally, the Dayaks can quite easily admit God—and not just one God, with His jealousy stressed in an attempt to save the face of their logic, but attended by as large a pantheon as spiritual fancy or convenience of worship dictate.

The weakness of the Dayak theory is the problem it leaves regarding the nature of the force in things. What is it like? Can it begin working of its own accord? Can it wax and wane? Does it continue to exist after the thing it has been in is destroyed? The problem is one which admits, and receives, many answers.

But generally it receives no answer at all, because the Dayaks do not bother about it. Concerning most ordinary everyday things, they think quite unsentimentally and 'scientifically'. They do not expect the stones to rise from the ground to strike them, and they do not consider the blades of grass on which they step. But if they do have cause to think about the force in things, which the bias of their thought inclines them to believe is there, they may conceive it as like the human self, or, to use the term often applied to this conception, they may conceive it as animistic. Now they do not always do so. It is important that we understand when they do so, the degree to which they do so, and why they do so. Otherwise we are likely to think them too different from ourselves, and we may put quite the wrong value on many of their statements, particularly some of those in Raseh's story.

The Dayak animism is of two degrees. The first degree concerns inanimate objects which are of constant interest to the people. The force in these objects is conceived merely as part of their nature, as it is theoretically part of the nature of everything, and is not generally thought of as free or as immortal. But it may be strong or weak, it may wax or wane, and its power is open to influence. For this reason the forces of bathing places, of hearths, of soap, of fields, and of other meaningful things may be named in religious invocations in the hope that they may be strengthened by the honourable mention made of them.

The second degree of animism is shown mainly in regard to plants. Here the Dayaks are faced with the problem of immortality. The force in plants is clearly a self-developing one. What happens, therefore, when the plant is destroyed? The force may go on the loose. The Dayaks are fairly sophisticated on this question, or at least their leaders in thought are. They do not hold for certain that there is a free floating force from destroyed plants. But they take no risks. If our mode of thought makes us pragmatists, theirs makes them precautionists. Thus at the times of their largest festivals they give offerings to the life forces of the grass and the trees cut down to make their paddy fields, forces which might be vindictive towards the crops planted in their stead.

We now have the clue to the true place of animism in Land Dayak thought. Animism flourishes where the emotions dwell. It sucks its strength from hope, fear and fancy. We said before that the Dayaks do not usually consider the blades of grass on which they tread. But they do consider, collectively and on special occasions, those they destroy in that centre of their hope and worry—their paddy fields. With especial tenderness they consider the vital force of the paddy itself, nursing it with ritual from the time it is seed until it is bowing down with ripened ears, and storing the harvested grain in semi-sacred bins—but always with something like half-belief, as insurance rather than as necessity.

So much for hope and fear. In the story which is to come we are concerned with fancy. There we shall see its effect in giving animistic quality to many things which in ordinary life would have it at most in low degree. The hero influences all kinds of things, from day and night to maiden's desire, by means of his mysterious medicines which have highly potent force. His fighting knives have wonderful power. He can make honey-trees dance.[1] But we must never forget, in reading the story, that we are in the exciting world of fancy and not in the world of everyday things. There are some cases of animism, however, which may be more directly accounted for in terms of the everyday world and its logic.

Now we are back to the log. There are three objects which are regarded in much the same way by the people of Mentu Tapuh.

---

[1] They are *tapang* trees. We call them honey-trees, because it is as a source of honey that they are most celebrated by the Land Dayaks. The bees hive in their lofty branches.

The other two are stones, to which stories also attach. Why should these objects be regarded animistically? They are not like paddy plants, or bathing places, or something hard to make and delightful to use like soap, on which the emotions centre. They are not fanciful. Their nature is common, although they are outstanding examples of it.

The attention paid to them becomes understandable if we see them as especial instances of the idea of force in things. The Dayak symbolization of abstract ideas is often more substantial than ours. It relies less on words and more on example. And so these especial instances, made influential by veneration, support a basic principle of Dayak thought.

We may thus view all the instances of animism which we have discussed as conceived in a union of logic and emotion, with religion the foster-parent. We cannot prove our view. But unless we hold it, or find a better one, we must fall back on the idea that the Land Dayaks are children. Some of them are children, and charming children too, but I found none above the age of twelve or so.

This has been a long exploration. Now that we are back on the direct track, we had better hurry along to the third class of story, in case we yield to the temptation to stray again.

The stories which we are putting into this third class are those which entertain only. They may be long, or they may be short. Many of them are simple tales for children. But in order to give a truthful idea of the range of Land Dayak stories, it is better that we choose as our example of this class one which is definitely unsuitable for children, although children are not kept away. It concerns that popular hero of so many stories, the mouse-deer, a little creature famous in life for his nimble ways and in fiction for his cheeky cunning.

One morning when the mouse-deer was skipping along through the jungle, he came upon the lair of a clouded leopard. In the lair was a young leopard cub. As the mother leopard seemed safely out of sight, the mouse-deer began to tease the cub, saying: 'What a dirty animal you are! Look at the black spots you've got all over you.' The cub began to cry. 'Why are you so filthy?' went on the mouse-deer. 'Doesn't your mother ever wash you?' 'Just wait till mummy comes back,' sobbed the cub, 'and I tell her what you've said. Then she will eat you.' 'When mummy comes back, I will assault her,' replied the mouse-deer. The form of the proposed assault was stated quite bluntly, but delicacy demands that it be left to our imaginations which, truly civilized, have no need of plain talk. The mouse-deer had barely uttered his boast when around the side of the lair came the mother leopard, having heard it. She pounced upon the mouse-deer. He jumped away, and raced off into the jungle, with the leopard hot upon him. In a moment he reached a hollow log, into which he ran. The leopard charged in after him, but the opening was so narrow that her head stuck fast in it. Coming out the other end of the log, the mouse-deer strolled casually back along the top of it, and proceeded to carry out his threat upon the leopard, powerless to resist.

This tale is funny because it is improper. It is improper even to us. But just how much more improper, and therefore more funny, it is to the Land Dayaks we cannot appreciate until we know of a peculiar idea they have regarding animals. They believe that it is dangerous to laugh at them. Near Mentu Tapuh there are some great caves, now giving a rich yield of edible birds' nests for sale to the Chinese. The limestone formations in these caves are believed to be the remains of a former village. It is said that once upon a time a visitor came to this village together with his hunting dog. As a practical joke, his host served him, as meat to go with his rice, some lumps of rubber. The dog grabbed one of these lumps, and getting his teeth stuck in it, ran about the longhouse yelping. The people laughed. Immediately a tremendous storm arose, and the village and everyone in it, including the visitor and his dog, were changed into stone.

One afternoon when I was in Mentu Tapuh a strange, short storm—perhaps it was a small whirlwind—struck the village, lifting half the roof off my house and blowing down several trees nearby. Villagers blamed it on to the fact that in the morning a dog, trying to steal some rice, had got its head stuck in a jar, and, as it ran around with the jar on its head, two small boys, now in disgrace, had laughed at it. Dogs are not helped by this peculiar belief. Dayaks argue that it is safest to be always angry with them.

It is enough to make a cat laugh—so runs our saying. A Dayak cat may laugh, but woe may betide a Dayak who laughs at it. This is the naughtiest thing of all to do. Children sometimes told to shake hands with the cat at my house, as they entered, would behave just as if they were up to mischief—giggles, nudges, avoidances, and little acts of boldness. To tell them to do so was, of course, behaviour more befitting a mouse-deer, and it was perhaps because of it that this particular house of all the houses in the village had to be singled out to lose its roof.

Even some mechanical toy animals, when first shown to a large gathering of fascinated children, were gazed upon with glee suppressed to the faintest rustle, until the old headman came in and, seeing them, laughed. Then a mighty gust of laughter, released at once from every throat, almost removed the roof again.

After cats come dogs, a close second on the gravity scale. Leopards and mouse-deer are far below, but are still on the scale. Therefore when the Dayaks find the above tale funny, they are being doubly naughty.

★   ★   ★

When Raseh spoke of his story, I thought that it would belong to this third class—a simple, ordinary story coming in whole or part from his own fertile imagination. In fact, it is a traditional tale of the Land Dayaks. Furthermore, amongst such tales it takes pride of place, not only because it is the longest and the most full of incident, but because it describes the ritual of the Festival of the Heads, regarded as the highest of the Land Dayak festivals, which are rated according to the type of offerings given, because human heads honour the gods most of all. There may, of course, be an origin-story for the ritual of the heads as well, but, if so, nobody in Mentu Tapuh seems to know it, and today the story which is given here serves as the main record for the people of the details of ceremonies now in eclipse.

Except perhaps in the wording of the songs, the story is not Raseh's creation. And since one of the reasons for songs in stories is the aid they give to memory even these may not be in any large part his invention. It is his story only in the sense that he remembers it best, and can tell it best. Great credit is due to him, however. Many persons have heard it, and enough remember different parts of it to serve as a check on Raseh's imagination, but only he remembers it as fully. His feat is considerable, because opportunities for hearing the story are limited. Like all the longer traditional tales, it is usually told in the fields, as the men and women weed the paddy, and the only time when story-telling—as distinct from irrepressible gossip—may take place in the paddy fields, if risk of harm to the paddy is to be avoided, is during the period between the end of the first weeding and the beginning of the harvest, a period when work is at its least urgent. Raseh was being most kind in offering to tell me the story in my house, and not in the hot sun on a hillside, or cramped in a paddy field shelter, waiting for the rain to stop.

Had I known all this about the story, I should not have treated

Raseh's first offer to tell it so lightly. Luckily he persisted, saying that we should hold over the question of payment until afterwards. So the telling began.

On each of the evenings a small group gathered in my house. We began late, after most people had gone to bed, so as not to be disturbed by too many. The group was made up of Minin, the son of the headman, who was a lesser authority on the story; Lutong, the father of Raseh and the second most celebrated priest of the ancestral cult; and a few others, some of whom had heard the story before. As it was told, I took it down on my typewriter, almost exactly as it is given now. The translation was checked at all doubtful points by talking it over with Nyandoh, the very clever young villager who helped me in all my work, and who knew simple English. The only parts really difficult to translate were the songs. The Land Dayaks have a special song language made up of a blend of Sea Dayak, Malay, and Land Dayak words of differing dialects, the particular blend in any case depending upon the genius of the author and the needs of rhyme, rhythm and assonance. In the case of ordinary songs, the range of words used is known well enough to keep reason peaceful under poetry's spell, but Raseh's songs were more erudite, and required explaining, to other listeners a little and to me a lot.

None of us were passive listeners. If we wanted to know why something was done, or how it was done, or what else had been done to make it possible, we asked. Questioning always takes place when tales are told in the village, and it serves to keep the telling lively. Its absence may explain why tales collected from a lone informant out of the story-telling atmosphere sometimes make rather dull reading.

The story took nine nights to tell. It is supposed to take that long, but from the length it occupies here it may seem surprising that it did. Two facts must be borne in mind. One is that the teller of the tale must sing all the songs, and Land Dayak singing is, on the whole, slow. Secondly, whereas we have given each song only once and merely mentioned its being sung again, Raseh sang it fully every time, the singing being a principal attraction of the story, and the more familiar the songs become the more they are enjoyed. Here we are in fact passing off as a narrative what was really a one-man opera. It may be noted, too, that we have not repeated the account of similar incidents. Thus, when the hero makes love to a second woman, we say ' . . and the same things happened as before', whereas Raseh told us again just what those things were. The story belongs to a world nearly free of strangers and quite free of books. There was no need for haste in the telling of it, for who would wish the excitement to end?

Actually there was one person who did wish it—Raseh's wife. This was the best time of the year for fishing at night on the river with spear and lamp, and she thought that Raseh should be catching fish for his family instead of telling tales. The crisis was overcome by my offering him a tin of fish, although by mistake he took the tin containing my supply of dried milk powder, which apparently satisfied his family—resigned to the fact that the fish, like everything else European, was liable to be peculiar.

We all enjoyed the story. When it was done, I offered Raseh the ten dollars. He refused it. He did not say that my need was greater than his, because that would have been manifestly untrue. Nor did he say, 'No thank you', for the Land Dayaks have no word equivalent to our common 'thank you' because, unlike Europeans, they do not expect a tribute in return for every little act of kindness they do. He simply said, 'No', wishing, now that I had heard the story and realized its worth, not to obscure the fact that he had never valued his performance simply in terms of cash. I did realize this fact very well. Raseh is an artist—in story, in song, and in dance. He takes what prizes he can thereby. But at heart he is always more than a commercial artist.

I forget how we settled the matter in the end.

THE LAND DAYAKS

I

THE LAND DAYAKS

THE fascination of Borneo for an anthropologist lies in the wide variety of peoples he may find there. They may all be sprung from a common stock—not far back in history as physical variations go—but in ways of life and even more in character they may differ much. Living for long with one of the groups may cause the others to pale into dullness. Knowing the Land Dayaks, I now believe that they are the finest people in Borneo, and also that their élite live in Mentu Tapuh. Other anthropologists who have lived elsewhere and do not know them might think otherwise. But the fact remains that the anthropologist first coming to Borneo has many different groups of people from which to choose. If he is lucky enough to stay in Borneo long enough to be able to make a second study, his interests may soon become absorbed by new friends. Only if he has had the fortune to be first with the Land Dayaks will he be disturbed every now and then, and for ever, by twinges around the heart.

In all this variety the best-known people are the Sea Dayaks, because they are the largest group, numbering in Sarawak about 190,000. They should not be confused with the Land Dayaks, a smaller but more anciently Bornean group numbering in Sarawak about 40,000. The respective names of the groups provide no clue to their differences, for both live inland along the rivers, the Sea Dayaks mainly in the Second and Third Divisions of Sarawak and the Land Dayaks entirely in the First Division.

The main difference is in the personal natures of the two peoples. Here it is dangerous for me, knowing only one of them well, to attempt a detailed comparison. But on appearances the Sea Dayaks are a confident people, masters—although not always wise masters since they sometimes waste the soil—of their environment, boastful but bold, and restless innovators for gain, prestige, or sheer enjoyment of change. In the past they have certainly been aggressive. Arriving in Sarawak probably only a few centuries ago, they spread rapidly, not through an entirely empty land but by pushing the peoples already there back from their ruined villages and their dead. Today their mode of life resembles in many outward respects that of other indigenous groups, but it is possible that many of their ways were acquired from these groups. It has even been said that they learnt the practice of head-hunting from the Land Dayaks. If so, they must have been extraordinarily apt pupils for they soon far outrivalled their teachers, practising their craft upon them.

We can leave the Sea Dayaks at this stage. The brief comment on their nature is relevant because it may help to explain the growth of a contrary nature in the Land Dayaks. The Land Dayaks suffered severely in the past from the Sea Dayaks. They are not at all confident. If they are stubborn, it is because they are defensive. They are quite sure that they are not masters of their world, because they know too well that there are others stronger who may invade it or who control it—not only the Sea Dayaks, although they are the worst, but Malays, who long exploited them as overlords, and the British, whose welcome peace seemed so unshakeable until the Japanese shook it. New menaces now trouble their sky—the Communists and the Indonesians from across the border. It is no wonder that they have vaguer fears as well— of natural catastrophe, of disease, and of demons in the countryside.

Nor are the Land Dayaks boastful. Visitors to them, who have known other peoples in Sarawak, are often struck by their modest quietness. The reason is simple. They believe they have nothing to boast about. They are a people without illusions—a fact which makes the task of a field-worker studying their ways hard at first, because the people, believing their culture of no importance in the world at large, do not think about its features in an abstract way. One cannot therefore readily learn the ideal pattern of conduct. Much more than with some peoples, one must just wait to see what happens, and then construct the pattern oneself. Any single villager is, of course, likely at times to entertain his pretensions, but if he shows much tendency to display them he is likely to be laughed at, and he is quite likely to come to laugh at himself.

A developed awareness of the funny side of things, always subtle and tuned by mood, extends much further. It is a quality in the people which a stranger may miss, because they are humorists rather than comedians, and in the presence of the stranger they may be far less than gay. They may be positively glum, with vacant eyes, staring indefatigably, serving as windows for appraising minds. Surprise awaits one who does miss the quality, for the Land Dayaks may extend their humour into the most sacred fields. No sense of reverence accompanies their religious ceremonies. A priest may interrupt his invocations to make a joke, and he may on occasion do his best to persuade the stranger to mimic him, to the great delight of all present. In some of the largest ceremonies nearly every serious episode is followed by a comic counterpart, sometimes carried out with almost as much apparent seriousness. If sorcery ritual is performed—which is rarely, and always against persons in other villages—it is in an atmosphere of suppressed glee at the wiles used to entrap the souls of the victims. It may be agreed, therefore, that when one day I saw a very small boy setting off with a catapult to pester sparrows, and asked him where he was going, and he replied, with scarcely a flicker of face, 'To hunt the largest species of hornbill'—the biggest bird in the jungle, and the hardest to catch—he was just displaying a trait typical also of his elders.

The humour is ironic, with an edge not bitter but deflating. It debunks the proud and reduces the great. Thus it is not only a protection for their extremely democratic society. It is a protection also against superior outsiders. It enables the people to turn a would-be mental defeat into something like a mental victory. It is not a conscious device, of course. It is a perspective on life, sharpened by adversity—a perspective as right as any—and one which gives enjoyment through seeing things that way.

Because of its subtlety, I am overstressing this trait by describing it. But its presence is real, and is obvious in the story which follows. The giants are enormous, but they are humiliated in a ridiculous way. Much more fun is had at the expense of the Malays, a people upon whom the Land Dayaks depended for trade but who, as their political masters, often exploited them by power and witchcraft. The hero, told by an excited villager that the Malay warriors are approaching, remarks contemptuously, 'Don't fuss! The Malays are always coming here to hawk salt, and to sell us this and that.' Then, Drake-like, he proceeds to take a bath. Later, when the Malays launch a second river-Armada, it is composed of boats of brass. Only a people as wealthy as the Malays could make such boats. But the boats clank so much against one another that the villagers are warned of their coming.

So much, then, for this trait. We have suggested its role in the story. Perhaps it is as well that no Europeans figure there. Once when misfortune struck my own boat, I had the uneasy feeling that the village chief and all the others in it dried out the quicker through being warmed by the thought that I was in it also. To see our story in its setting, or at least in the setting in which it is told, we need to turn for a while from the character of the people to sketch their general way of life, especially insofar as it bears on the story.

II

THE COUNTRYSIDE AND THE JUNGLE

A HUNDRED years ago old jungle covered most of the rolling land around the site where Mentu Tapuh now stands. Three miles upstream, the village of Mentu, of which Mentu Tapuh was to be an offshoot, must already have been inhabited for a long time, for today no tradition survives of an earlier ancestral home, the people believing that their ancestors emerged naked from a cave nearby and built Mentu as their first village. But until a hundred years ago or less the inhabitants of the village were never more than a small group of frontiersmen on the edge of a far-spreading forest. In the following years they were joined by migrants from the denser Land Dayak populations lying to their west and south. Their numbers also probably grew through natural increase when the White Rajah's peace robbed disease of its ally in war. More and more land was cleared. Mentu Tapuh was established and today much of the old forest in its neighbourhood has given way to a tangle of secondary growth, denser on the ground but more open to the sky. This is the 'countryside', where the farms are made. It is very different from the jungle. The sun smiles on it. It is not very frightening. But it is lonely.

The countryside is not quite all dense with the tangle of secondary growth. Some of it is green with paddy. Some of the rest, which was green with paddy last year, is now covered only with grass, waist-high. But beneath the grass the bamboo, shrubs and vines will be rising, soon to make these old fields like most of the countryside all the time, for only a little of it is cultivated at once, and that little changes in place from year to year. Every June each village family will clear one or two new fields, covering together an area of from two to four acres. The tangled growth on the chosen area is cut down, and burnt when it is dry. The seed is put in, the plants tended, and the harvest gathered. Thereafter, a few fields, or parts of fields, may be used for a year or two longer as sugar-cane or cassava gardens, but most of the clearings will be given up, for ten years or so, to the lush, wild, overwhelming weeds. The farmer is glad to see these weeds take possession quickly, for if they do not, and only choking *lalang* grass springs up instead, he knows that he can never farm in that place again.

Yet the sight touches the soul. For a whole season all one's interests have centred in the field. One has walked there in the dawn, and home again in the late afternoon. One has worked there in the sun, gossiping with helpers, blackened the girls in the working-party with charcoal on the day of the burning, laughed with gaily-dressed companions on the happy planting-day, feasted with the gods there, worried over the paddy's health, fearing rats, or grubs, or blight, or storm, or flood, and gathered the harvest, despondently or with gratification. And now one must turn away from the field to face another year in quite another place.

I say it touches the soul. But the Dayaks say it may separate the soul from the body. Therefore, at the yearly festival after the harvest is stored, they summon back souls which may still be wandering in fields now given up. They call them back home—back to the village, crowded, noisy with cocks and pigs and children, contrasting so comfortingly with the quiet, overgrown countryside.

The primary jungle—we would call it primeval had the word not become spoilt with too much use, because it conveys well the feeling the jungle gives rise to—has been pushed back, but still not very far. From the north it sends out a broad tongue along a high limestone ridge right into the village sky, and from the base of this tongue, a mile or two away, it widens out into a forest hundreds of square miles in extent, the last great area of jungle in this part of Borneo and now declared a reserve by the Government, which is anxious about the watershed of the Sadong river.

The jungle is very different from the countryside. Everyone is deeply aware of it, perhaps most of all those who keep away from it. To try to understand the attitudes of the Land Dayaks, I believe that one must do more than study their economy, their politics, their mating and breeding habits. One should go into the jungle, quite often and sometimes alone. It is fascinating to wander in it, and a relief to come out. It is well, however, not to go so far in as to deny oneself the pleasure of this relief. The jungle is very deceitful, duplicating what seem at first to be singular features in a way so confusing that one may quickly be like the hero of our Story 'walking on and on, for ever walking uphill and downhill, on hills of a thousand different kinds'.

It is true that one is not likely to go on wandering for ever. The Dayaks have a clever way of seeking those who have gone astray. Search-parties set out in various directions beating the big brass festival gongs to guide the wanderer towards them. But they are not silly enough to begin searching until it has become clearly necessary, and the night or two which one may spend in the jungle in the meantime, sodden and bitten and frightened by the hints of inhuman company, may not be worth the vivid impression they will undoubtedly give. To be lost is one of the greatest fears of the Land Dayaks. There are some bold hunters in Mentu Tapuh, who range far, but they are only two or three. Most men rarely go far from the tracks or nearer stream-beds, although in parties, which sometimes may be made up mainly of women, they may go further to collect rattan vine. Practically and emotionally, the jungle means much to the Land Dayaks, and a great part of its emotional meaning is fear.

The jungle has, of course, many delights, which differ according to time, to place and to person. Anyone, Dayak or European, is probably elated by the early morning valleys, with a whole day of light ahead, when the birds and the gibbons are calling. The woman gathering rattan may be gladdened by finding a length with the sections five hand-spans apart, the Dayak equivalent of a four-leaved clover, but more useful since it can make an elegant staff for an old man. The pig-hunter may be excited by fresh tracks. For myself at least, there were many lovely glades where the butterflies, or *teribomban* as the Dayaks called them, not recognizing the killing-bottle, played, some of them small and some fit to be classed as birds, their miraculously-coloured wings perfect or so tattered by life as to make their agile flying another miracle.

But delight is not the most constant feeling in the denser jungle. There is a heightened sensibility and a wariness. Exuberance is out of place in the presence of much that is bigger, and so much that is other, than man. In the silent and ancient shade, the fallen trunks, the moist, rough carpet of decay; the endless limited vegetable views, growth upon growth, of trees and vines and ferns glossy on top but hooked barbarously beneath; the animal manifestations, there and gone or heard or only suspected—all these convey a sense of a life-force, or life-forces, apart from man, greater than him, inconsiderate of him, and amid which he upholds himself by his will and skill. The sense is a subtle one. No one takes the trees to be anything more than trees. A vine is but a vine, to be slashed if it is in the way. An animal is only an animal, to be killed if it is worth it. What counts is the total effect—and the sense of something more. For a European, city-coddled, the experience of the jungle is sobering, enlightening, and vaguely threatening. The Dayaks are already enlightened. They know that their place in total nature is small, however distinctive. Therefore they feel the threat more.

But can we say that they do feel this way about the jungle? Unless we are psycho-analysts, with a ready-made formula which explains everything but the content of people's thoughts, we can never be quite sure how anyone else thinks. But we do know that the Dayaks have fears of the jungle, and that these fears are irrational. They are irrational because they go far beyond proven facts.

There are, of course, some dangers in the jungle which are real. The spirit of an English wood is different from the spirit of the forest in Borneo, and the difference is partly due to the worse things in the latter. There are more poisonous snakes. One may not see them often, but there are stories about them. A man walking near Mentu Tapuh was sprung at by a large king-cobra. Its teeth caught in the long trousers he luckily was wearing. He seized it by its throat, and strangled it. I do not know whether this story is true, but everyone in the village says it is. One morning a woman came to me saying that she had been bitten by a snake. Her arm was swollen enormously. She said that on the previous evening when she had been walking home in the dusk from her paddy field, she saw the snake—of a kind easily seen because of its scarlet head and the scarlet tip to its tail. She cut off its head with her bush-knife. Knowing the snake was poisonous, she carried the head carefully to the side of the track to bury it. She returned to pick up the body of the snake to take it home to roast for supper. As she lifted it, she was bitten. Of course she did not stay to investigate, but the explanation on which everyone agreed was that when she had first come upon the scene one snake had been swallowing another. The head which she cut off was the head of the snake which was being swallowed, and in the dusk she did not notice that another head lay behind. While she was burying the cut-off head, the second head completed its swallowing and so was free to punish the hand which had robbed it of the upper part of its meal.

On another morning a man brought me the skin of a snake which he had killed near the village. It was a king-cobra. It measured thirteen feet, and the head was missing. I gave it to the Sarawak Museum, where I trust it is now on the wall as public testimony to the truth at least of this tale. A living specimen of one of the rarest and most interesting snakes in Borneo—the poisonous 'flying snake', which, launching itself from a tree, can glide up to fifty yards—was also intended by me for Mr Tom Harrisson at the Museum, but a python, which was put in the box with it, swallowed it on the way there.

Snakes, then, there certainly are. But although they add a little to the mistrust of the jungle, they do not explain it. The Dayaks know that the likelihood of harm from them is small. All except a mating king-cobra, and apparently also an occasional malicious one, will harm man only when he is in the way of their flight. During the lifetime of the oldest man in Mentu Tapuh, only three villagers have been killed by snakes. It is at night-time that the greatest fear of the jungle is felt, and then the danger from snakes is at its least, although we must note one widely-believed tale of a man who woke up to find himself inside a python. Fortunately he was wearing his knife in its sheath at his side, so he cut his way out. The slime on his body when he returned home proved the truth of his story. Snakes do figure in our story, but not as creatures of fear. The dreaded reptile is not a snake. It is a dragon. And there are no dragons in the jungle, although Lutong, the father of Raseh, swears that he saw one in the river, when he was fishing. It was twenty-four feet long, and glowed.

From other animals in the jungle there is even less danger. A bear may panic dangerously when cornered, but bears are rare, and a fearful person can refrain from cornering them. Clouded leopards, which are still rarer, have never, as far as I know, hurt anyone. The animal which is mentioned most in our story is the orang-utan. It, too, is a victim of man, not a menace to him. Or rather we had better say it could be a victim under different circumstances, for the orang-utan now enjoys privileged status in the jungle. Because the south-western part of Borneo and a small area in Sumatra are the only places in the world where this great ape is found, it has been placed under Government protection. The present generation of Land Dayaks, fully understanding the high importance of the species to overseas scientists, appreciate the need for this measure. Although their fathers and grandfathers regarded the animal as a legitimate prize of the hunt, and although they know it to be in such numbers that their occasional killings, as distinct from the depredations of European collectors, could not threaten it with extinction, they never now harm a hair on its back. They would swear to this fact, and I am prepared to swear with them. In any case, despite the formidable look of a large specimen, the orang-utan is harmless, and what Dayak would harm a harmless animal?

There is another ape in the jungle—the gibbon. It is fairly numerous and is not an uncommon item on Mentu Tapuh menus. The Dayaks recognize the likeness of both these apes to man, but from this likeness they draw a conclusion contrary to that of Darwin. The contrast in view shows how two authorities considering the same facts can deduce from them exactly opposite theories. The evolutionists say that man is an ascended ape; the Land Dayaks say that the ape is a descended man. The orang-utan, they say, spring from a man who, becoming ashamed at some misdeed in the village, ran away into the jungle. He stayed there so long that he took on the form of an orang-utan, and his children were like him. The wife, on this theory, is the missing link.

The gibbons had a different founder. He was a villager who differed from most men in that he was very fond of cooking, which meant that he spent a great deal of time bending over a smoky fire. One night he visited his beloved in her bed. When dawn came, he was horrified to see that she was black. He rushed to get a looking-glass, and was overcome with shame to realize that the black had come from his own body, which was irremediably encrusted with soot. He ran away into the jungle, where he clung to a branch in shame. He clung there so long that his arms stretched. He became the progenitor of the gibbons, which are black in colour and long-armed like himself. This theory is superior to that of Darwin in that it leaves no debate about the origin of differences of pigmentation amongst the primates.

This catalogue of animals is relevant to our Story, but none of them is dangerous enough to explain the anxiety felt in the jungle. The anxiety is about other things—about nature itself, and about supernatural beings. Neither grounds of fear would we admit as reasonable. Therefore the Dayaks by differing from us prove themselves irrational.

The peculiar and the great in nature are suspect, because they suggest a force, either perverted or exceedingly strong, which may act wantonly. A vine writhed fantastically may ensnare the soul of a person who crosses over it, or under it, or through its coils. Large trees may fall, or big rocks roll, to crush the passer-by. We, too, can accept the fact of such things happening. Why they should happen at one moment rather than another, or to one thing rather than another, we rarely know, but we are sure there is a cause, although we might be thoughtless enough to speak of an 'accident'. The Dayak view is rather different. A possibility of autonomy is allowed to the trees and the rocks. The risk from them is therefore greater than we might consider it.

There is a virtue in the Dayak view for one who wanders much in the jungle. We said that anyone might feel the jungle as vaguely threatening. The European, allowing nature no right of surprise, may have to move with his anxiety through the sombre entangled shadow, trying not to recognize his company. The Dayaks, by giving substance to their fears, can take action against them in advance.

The action which they do take is ritual, and this often means fun as well. At the times of the biggest festivals, an especially twisted vine is brought from the jungle to the longhouse verandah. Maidens dance around it with fighting knives, leap over it, and finally sever it, thus robbing such vines of their power to ensnare souls. This is psychological reassurance. It counteracts the formation of concepts of danger when one is in the jungle. More regularly morale is boosted on most of the many occasions when invocations are made to the ancestral spirits. Amongst other evil influences against which the priest prays are listed '. . . the cry of the vine, the twisted and knobbly vine; the thunder clap; the falling of the dead tree; the big rocks turning over; the stones tumbling down'. Trouble is not to be expected from them after they have been spoken to in this fashion.

But direct anxiety about nature is always a vague worry, hardly crossing the threshold of consciousness except at prayer-time, or when an excuse is needed for a festival episode, or when blame is to be laid for a happening already over, or perhaps when one is deep in the far jungle. Much more vivid is the fear of demons, demons who may be met with anywhere in the jungle but whose commonest dwelling-places are the banks of streams, the swampy places where the growth is stunted and the ground thick with roots, and on hilltops.

The story regarding these beings, whom we are calling 'demons' for want of a better name, states that once upon a time there were two kinds of people both created by the supreme god, or 'origin-spirit'. They were constantly quarrelling with each other, so the supreme god decided that they should live apart and that one kind should be invisible to the other. The invisible group, which by 1951 had separated into many different tribes each with its own peculiar characteristics, are the demons. As if to compensate for the advantage which their invisibility gave them over ordinary men, the god decreed that

demons troubling man must call off their attacks if they were fed and
fêted.

Therefore all Dayak festivals are to a large extent parties put on for the
demons. For all the days and nights of the festival, the big brass gongs
should be kept booming out over the countryside inviting all
mischievous, malicious and resentful beings in the neighbourhood
to come up on to the longhouse verandah to see the dancing, to eat
the delicacies, to drink the wine. Then, in a final ceremony when
exhaustion has brought the fun to an end, they are sped on their way,
quite impolitely since they are under an obligation to go, but with
enough provisions to sustain them on what they are told should be a
very distant journey. The village is thus cleansed of harmful influences—
until such time as the desire of the villagers, their food supplies, their
freedom from pressure of work, or an event of outstanding happiness
or unhappiness, suggests a further round of merry-making.

The festivals and the group of people living together—since a
crowd frightens the big demons—cast a kind of *cordon sanitaire* around
the village. The demons most to be dreaded are those who dwell
beyond this cordon and who have not attended the parties. They are
to be met with in the distant countryside and particularly in the
deep jungle. They are of many kinds. Those who play a main part
in our Story are enormous, which is the reason why we have translated
the word *antu*—the generic term for demons—as 'giant'. Other
demons may appear as fierce animals. Some are seductresses, who
lure men into love and then consume the means by which they express
it. Lahot in Mentu Tapuh is said to have met such demons. They were
three beautiful girls who led him back to their longhouse. It was a
longhouse which looked exactly like his own, so that had he not been
a wary young man he would have been deceived into thinking that
he was being entertained safely in his own home. When they were
in the house, the girls began to show their fondness for him, but he
delayed the introductions by saying—the Dayaks being frank in
such matters—that he wished to urinate. Once outside he hastened
beneath the longhouse, quickly piled rubbish against its supports and
set it alight, cremating his would-be mistresses.

With such demons about it is no wonder that many persons fear to
go far in the jungle. The timid and the children prefer to stay at home
altogether. Others of those whose business takes them into the jungle
enter with the urge to get out again as soon as possible. But how, may
we ask, can even the boldest dare to venture into notorious demon

country? The answer lies in the true nature of the demons. We have not yet fully explained it. To give a form to our coming explanation, we may hint now that the country the demons really live in is the country of the mind, and the laws they obey are those of the imagination.

The demons are not spirits—immortal, after-worldly, insubstantial, and invulnerable. They are creatures like man, bound like him to the mortal cycle of birth, marriage, child-bearing, and death, and having the same kinds of weaknesses. Thus they are not inevitably beyond human power. Man can escape them, beat them, cheat them—if he is fast enough, strong enough, or clever enough. Some demons can apparently use their cloak of invisibility, or change their shape, at will. They may display superhuman strength. They seem able to be here, there, and somewhere else the next moment. Yet despite these powers which should make them invincible, men believe that they can protect themselves against them.

Some of the means of defence are reasonable, as for instance the use of charms, or spells, or incense, or, most potent of all, a skew-cross set at the mouths of tracks or in fields. The Dayaks fear or dislike certain things, so it is reasonable that the demons should also have their own fears and dislikes. Other means of defence are ethical, and so we must commend them. Certain tribes of demons are in effect policemen. They punish those who break the village code, or punish the associates of the breakers. Laduh, we saw, was struck because of something which he should not have done. There is one tribe which punishes idle gossip, although these must be a lax crowd. Another tribe punishes priests who miss out parts of their invocations. Grand-father Jon was struck dumb for half an hour for doing this, but his lapse was a particularly foolish one for it was the names of these demons themselves which he forgot.

Poisonous insects, which if not really demons are much like them, behave in the same way, especially scorpions and centipedes but also hornets. One should not tempt these insects, but one may not expect to get bitten unless one has been bad. An interesting case was that of Tuntong, a young boy from the village of Suhu who was staying with me in Mentu Tapuh. In his village there is an unhygienic prohibition on the washing of mats. I asked him to wash my mat. He said it was wrong. I pointed out that he was in Mentu Tapuh not in Suhu. As he was a very kind boy, he washed it. Unfortunately when he sat down after his labours, he sat on top of a hornet, which stung him embarrassingly. The headman of Mentu Tapuh told him that it was his own fault for breaking the laws of the village to which he belonged. Tuntong could have fined me for egging him on. On another occasion I was myself stung by two hornets in my bed after the old men had warned me of the danger of allowing children to beat on tins in my house in imitation of gongs when it was not festival time. This was strange, because none of the men had been near my sleeping place! Thereafter I always had my house cleansed along with the others at the times of the festivals.   .

One insurance against demons, therefore, is to be good. We must note, however, that demons are anywhere likely to be capricious. They are alleged to have given the Catholic missionary dysentery, when by rights they should have left a distinguished visitor alone. And in the jungle they may be terrible individualists, admitting no law but their own evil.

It is the purely physical means of defence which strike us as unreasonable, because they are used against beings who are not constrained by physical laws. People may believe, for instance, that they could fight demons. In truth they would not try if they met one. They would certainly run as fast as their legs would carry them. But still they trust that human legs may outrace creatures to whom in other contexts they may impute the power of flying. This is not a logical belief. Of course it is not, because the demons are illogical. That is half the trouble with them. The Dayak defence against them is their own form of what the Christians would call faith, expressed in terms of direct action or ritual. One of the great benefits of our Story to the villagers is the bolstering which their faith gets from it. The hero outwits or slays every demon, no matter how big.

Now let us touch wood and then assert that the demons as the Dayaks conceive them are not real. We need to do so for the sake of our argument. We suggested that the fears of the jungle arose from its total effect—and the sense of something more. If the demons are not real but are simply the particular substances the Dayaks give to their fears then there must be this vaguer awareness, or something like it, enlivening their imaginations.

The Dayaks do not press their symbolizations of the jungle's threats too far. As we saw, they leave their demons illogical. We may not take the same view as to what there is in the jungle. But it behoves us not to disregard demons altogether. Created in our own classical past, one at least stalks along with us, especially in the Colonies. He is

Hubris. He may do no more than lead us firmly back home. But he may strike deeply, although, like Dayak demons, he may leave no marks on the surface of our bodies.

There is another class of beings haunting the jungle whom we have not yet mentioned. They are called *pinyamun*. Their supernatural abilities put them on the same mental plane as demons, but theoretically they are men. They are supposed to be head-hunters on the hunt. The Land Dayaks say they are Sea Dayaks from the Saribas river region. Other groups in the country will claim that the danger comes from hunters of different origin, for the belief in the threat is common to all native groups. Every now and then some incident will set off an alarm, and then a ripple of fear runs over a sizeable area of Sarawak. The incidents are always slight.

It may be that a stray anthropologist looks too obviously at the cranial features of his hosts. Twice Mentu Tapuh shivered while I was there, although not from this cause. The first time was when a headless body was discovered by the police at a place down on the coast several days' journey away. It turned out afterwards that a fellow-villager had shot another accidentally, and then had decapitated him to bury the head elsewhere in the hope that the victim would not be identified as the man with whom he had gone hunting. The second scare arose over a survey for a proposed bridge across the Sadong river. It was said that the engineer had employed Sea Dayaks to collect a Land Dayak head with which to appease the river spirits for the disturbance they would suffer from the building of the bridge, the Land Dayaks being naive enough, still, to believe that a survey is a prelude to action.

Once the fear begins to spread, it infects everyone—not only the Land Dayaks but the Chinese and Malays as well, while the District Officer becomes anxious about the anxiety all around him. But it is the Land Dayaks who suffer most acutely. Rumours fly from ear to ear of apparitions here, there and everywhere. The head-hunters are really demons in a new guise. Why they so readily take on this guise is not hard to understand. It is not only because of the long tradition of heads truly lost. The head-hunters are the bogey men of the Land Dayaks. Little children who wander far from their mothers' backs are warned that they lie in wait for them. As these children grow up, any ventures beyond the ordinary continue to take them mentally into the head-hunters' range.

During a scare, it is believed the head-hunters may be met with in the open countryside. One should go abroad only with others, and always carry a weapon. But not, of course, for attack. The Land Dayaks prefer to have their fights in phantasy. The hero of our Story slays head-hunters as easily as he slays demons. That is why he is a hero. It is far better to leave the task to him.

When there is no scare on, a person can feel reasonably safe in the countryside. But he can never be certain about the jungle. Head-hunters may appear there without warning. The jungle is generally a much worse place than the countryside. In the jungle the loneliness felt is the loneliness of humankind in an inhuman world of life. The sense of self is heightened by the contrast, and the village is seen as a dear place of alliance against so much. Grown Land Dayaks do not walk in dread in the jungle. It would not be fair to say that they did. The majority of men may feel nothing more than a vague unease, quite dispersed in daylight hours if others are near. But all persons prefer to get back to the village, with its company, sooner rather than later, and think it by far the best place in all the jungle and all the countryside.

III

THE VILLAGE

UNLIKE many Europeans, the Land Dayaks do not actually share their homes with the larger domestic animals. They do, however, have pigs and fowls which spend a good deal of time underneath the longhouses, supplementing otherwise scanty meals with scraps and refuse dropped through the floor-slats by the residents above. The pigs also include in their diet such human waste as descends from the longhouse, although in Mentu Tapuh, as distinct from many other Land Dayak villages, it is generally considered that the proper place for the disposal of such waste, at least in daylight hours, is in the river. Tuntong, from Suhu, thought this was a dirty habit. When he visited the coast, and found that the sea was salty, he held that the Mentu Tapuh people and others like them were responsible.

It is because of the pigs that the village area is bare of grass, being hard clay in the sun and half a quagmire when it rains. It is far from bare of other things. Decaying fronds from palms planted indiscriminately throughout the village, putrid coconut shells, rotting bamboo cast away by workers on the houses, all kinds of rubbish too hard for the pigs to eat, lie scattered profusely everywhere. A European, used probably to places which other people tidy for him, may find the scene hard to stomach if he knows he has to live in it. With his developed germ-theory and his prejudices strong upon him, he is not likely to appreciate the abandoned beauty of it all, or to understand the town-quality which the cluttering-up gives to the village in the eyes of its people.

Impelled by his first impression, he may protest. Whereupon the following conversation will ensue:

> 'Your village is dirty.'
> 'It is filthy.'
> 'Why don't you clean it up?'
> 'We like it the way it is.'
> 'The rubbish is unhealthy.'

'The pigs feed better in it.'
'It breeds mosquitoes.'
'Nonsense. Have you never been in the jungle,
and seen the mosquitoes there?'

And the people are right. There are hordes of mosquitoes in the
jungle and countryside, and fairly few in the village. Most villagers
do sleep under mosquito-nets, but the nets are desired as much for the
privacy they give in common household rooms as for comfort.

This conversation would take place only when it was understood
to be an exchange of opinion with plain speaking on both sides. It
could well take place when a District Officer was speaking to the
people, but not if he were actually reprimanding them for the state
of the village. They would know him to be speaking with the authority
behind him of a Government with a fetish for tidiness. Therefore
they would give a different answer. They would promise to tidy
up the village on the morrow. The District Officer would have won
his point, and he could look forward to winning it again on his next
visit to the village, for probably the same rubbish would still be there.

The people would not have given their promise dishonestly. It is
probably true that the average Dayak is almost as capable of deceit,
although usually in a milder form, as the better-than-average European.
This is a harsh comment on the Dayaks, but if it must be made it is
best made now, because the case in question proves that the Dayaks
are often not deceitful when it looks as if they are. In the mood of the
meeting everybody would agree with what the speakers said. The
trouble would arise solely from the fact that it is easier to imagine
work than to do it. On the morrow, when reality summoned, quite a
number of persons would find the task on that particular day in-
convenient. Things nearer the heart would press to be done. They
would not turn up on the job. And no one could make them do so
if their minds became set against it, for the truth of the matter is that
the Land Dayaks are anarchists.

Perhaps anarchist is too strong a word, but the Land Dayaks
certainly do not live in one of those societies, existing in the minds
of theorists, in which individuality is sunk in the affairs of the tribe.
Theirs is a democratic society which at times bears out the worst
fears of Plato but which also has certain virtues too simple to be fully
appreciated in the sweep of a philosophic vision. Individuality may
sometimes be shown remarkably. Once in the village of Mentong

I saw one group of villagers, who had not yet finished their paddy harvesting, carrying out ritual to prolong the dry weather, while fifty yards away another group, who with their harvest over had been planting sugar-cane, were tinkling bowls to encourage rain, and neither group questioned the right of the other to try to bring to the countryside of both the kind of weather it wanted. This is an exceptional case, best explained by the fact that at heart the Dayaks are fatalists who do not expect much to come of efforts to sway nature. In practical affairs the people work in better with one another, but they do so from mutual interest and not because they are bound to a system or to rulers.

The Land Dayaks are anarchists to the extent that no one amongst them is strong enough to force the others to do anything which they do not wish to do. In their classless society there are no true chiefs. Each village has a headman, nowadays confirmed in office by the Government, but he leads only when the people agree to be led. The way he gets his office and the way he uses it ensure that he will not become a dictator.

Anyone stands a chance of becoming headman, although a relative of a previous good leader stands a slightly better chance, not so much because of the relationship itself but because he has been more in the public eye. Appointment is by common consent and except by mistake consent will not be given to a man who seeks to govern by his own will. The qualities which appeal are those which the people think will help themselves. They want a wise man, so that they can profit by his advice. They want him to be gentle, so that his advice will not be thrust upon them. They would prefer him to be rich, partly for the sake of village prestige, partly in the fond expectation that he will feed visitors at his cost and not at theirs, and partly in hope that his wealth-getting power will spread to them who are his people. If he is a priest it is a further advantage because of his influence with the ancestors. Finally, it is a great point in his favour if he stands well with the Government, for then he can check its interference and may even score a point or two over it. Grandfather Ichau, the headman of Mentu Tapuh, had all these qualities except the last, and the lack of that one did not matter because the people thought he stood as well with the Government as in fact he should have done.

The headman so appointed may have quite a lot of influence. Although he can lead only when the people wish to be led, he can, if he is careful, foster the wish in them. Issues of public interest are always considered by a general meeting, either in the headhouse or on the longhouse verandah, to which all may come who care to do so. In our Story, Gumiloh calls such a meeting to investigate a matter of seduction, perhaps with a premonition of the fate soon to befall her, but unless the issue is of a kind to concern them particularly, women do not usually take part in the meetings, although the opinions the men express at them will be governed to a large extent by the views the women have put forward in all the earlier talk in the houses and in the fields.

Generally it is the headman who calls the meetings as the demand or the need for them arises. He thus has an important role in making sure that the village attends to its business, but it is not a role which calls for great qualities of leadership because almost anyone could fulfil it. More positively, the tone of his opening remarks may in doubtful issues set the course of opinion one way or the other. But here too his influence is slight, for he rarely tries to be an advocate, knowing that mere primacy of argument can count for little in the long flow of talk which may run on through eddies of irrelevance and rapids of controversy for many enjoyable hours. His real leadership, if he has any, comes in another way, harder to see.

I watched Grandfather Ichau very carefully at a number of village meetings. I was puzzled as to why the outcome so often agreed with his own wishes, although he spoke very little. Then it dawned on me that this was just the reason why it did so. His leadership lay in what Trollope calls a *vis inertiae*.[1] Everyone else with views pressed them forcefully and often, for at the meetings all are free to speak. Grandfather Ichau chose his words carefully, left them unclouded by argument, said them at the right times, and kept them few. Thus his comments stood out, clear, as beacons in the general debate. When the people say they want their headman to be wise and gentle, they are picking out the very qualities most suited to give leadership in their assertive democracy.

The meetings always come to an agreed decision which everyone recognizes, although it may not be formally expressed. As this decision is accepted as right by everyone, we may call it unanimous, but we must be careful lest our use of this word delude us into thinking that Dayak democracy is a dull affair in which people never differ. The decisions should be thought of as unanimous in much the same way as is any decision of the British Parliament, and there may be as much

[1] Anthony Trollope, *Framley Parsonage.*

opposition *en route* to them, but without the last-ditch defiance of the lobby. The difference between the British and the Land Dayak systems is mainly that Dayak democracy is more liberal—using the word in its general, and not in its political sense. It is more liberal both in the way it treats opinion and in the way it governs action.

Strong opinions, if stuck to, will not be over-ridden. One single stubborn person can prevent an action which has the support of everyone else. In such a case the unanimity which closes the meeting is an agreement to do nothing. An instance occurred while I was in Mentu Tapuh. A proposal to convert a swampy, stagnant place in the village into a playing area was held up for a long time because one woman had one tree growing in the centre of it, and she refused to let it be rooted out. The tree was of the same ancient character as herself, long past fruiting. She was really objecting to a rooting-out of a little bit of the old order. At last, when she was offered six young trees to be planted for her in compensation, she wavered just long enough for the deed to be done, after which she was left prognosticating evil for her village and its desecrators. She was Laduh's grandmother.

Usually, however, the meeting does agree to do something. Obstinacy can give no political gain in the democracy because there are no parties, and therefore people sooner or later generally add their support to the prevailing view, thus not merely avoiding uncomfortable isolation but enjoying the pleasure of taking part in the formation of a popular decision. The positive unanimity so reached, however, may be of various shades, and according to its shade it will be variously compelling.

The reason for this lies in the fact that the greatest force controlling persons' actions in this society is public opinion. The Dayak democrats do not bow to it lightly, but they do not enjoy conflict with it, and the greater the conflict the less happy they are, although one or two, like Grandfather Ichau in episodes of his younger days when some said he sowed wild paddy, have proved on occasion remarkably tough. Now, the public debates not only argue out a common decision but they also let each person see just how strong is the support for it, and therefore how much disapproval he must face if he privately decides to do otherwise.

In the case of most schemes considered by meetings, such as preparations for festivals, the public heart is in them. In other cases, such as the initiation of the season's farming, persons accept the scheme for joint action because it involves work which they would have to do sooner or later anyway, and it is more enjoyable and convenient to do it together. Thus self-interest and public enthusiasm usually ensure that there are no absentees, unless with an unchallengeable excuse. This does not mean, of course, that things go smoothly. The Dayak canoe of state, as it sails along, often has as many claimants for the captaincy as there are crew. There is no discipline aboard and hence no mutiny. But, as the others argue, the true leaders thrust their paddles in and send the canoe wobbling towards its goal. In other words, the work gets done in the best possible way, because everyone feels he has had his say.

It is very different, however, with such a scheme as cleaning the village to suit the strange ideas of a peripatetic District Officer. Respect for him demands agreement. Agreement in all honesty demands a meeting. But in the morning when some turn up, others will not be there. Then those who are there refuse to do anything in the others' absence. They refuse self-righteously. They would, they say, be working not only for themselves but for others. It would be quite wrong to do other people's work without recompense. The reason for their strong moral feelings upon the issue should become clear in a moment. Actually they face a moral dilemma, because of the promise made. One time when I was present, this dilemma was solved by those who had turned up holding another meeting at which they delegated the task to the children. The children held a meeting, but some disappeared into the bush. With no one else to pass the work down to, the others let it rest.

Yet a Dayak cannot build his house alone, and he does not often work in his paddy field alone. He dislikes doing so, because, he says, 'the sun grows hot upon his back' if he is by himself. Even though the harvest will all be his, he generally has a number of people to help him. Now, surely, here is a contradiction. If group work for the benefit of one is the usual thing, persons on public works should not be so prickly about their individual rights. But there is no contradiction. The system of group work is such as to make it imperative for persons to be prickly about their rights.

Let us suppose that Laduh decides the time is ripe for another day's work on his paddy field. In the dawn, after his breakfast of boiled rice, or wild sago if his rice has run out, he goes to the paddy-stores, where he will meet other people. Perhaps he has already come to an arrangement with some of them on the previous evening in the longhouse, but others he will meet by chance. Everybody going to work likes to linger for a while at the paddy-stores, picking up the village news. It means to them what the morning newspaper means to the European, but is more sociable. Before setting off for the country-side it is pleasant to gossip a while, near the tall *durian* trees with their promise of a luscious November, in the fine morning—and it is always fine when one goes to work, because if it is wet one stays at home. Not that the Dayaks are sugar-babies. With nearly two hundred inches of rain a year, much of it with little warning, and with creeks and rivers and sweat, they are too often wet. But as children they are taught to avoid rain when they can. Especial warnings are given against sun-showers. These are called *ujan jala antu*, or 'the throwing-nets of the demons', and one must scutter away from beneath them.

During the gossiping, Laduh will invite other persons to spend the day working on his field. On ordinary days the number who do so may be anywhere from two to twenty. On the day of the planting it may be forty or more. Now, to each person who does work a day for him, Laduh will owe a day's labour in return. He need not pay it immediately. He may work his own field for two or three days at a stretch, doubling or trebling his debt. And he need not pay it himself. The paddy field, which we have been calling his, is not his alone. It is shared by all his household. Any member of his household may pay the debt he has acquired. His wife could do so, if he had one, or the uncle with whom he lives. Unfortunately his grandmother is too old to be of much use as a counter in the labour-exchange, but now and then she does a day's weeding for her household, or on its behalf.

The complications do not end here. While Laduh has been working on the household's field, other members of the household may have worked on the fields of different persons. These persons, who thus fall into the household's debt, may be called upon to pay the debts which Laduh acquires.

The result is that as the season advances Laduh's household becomes involved in a complex tally of debts and credits. They all must cancel out in the end, or else there will be a squabble, and the household has its reputation for future seasons to think of. And they must cancel out in such a way as to give the household the right amount of labour at the right times. Some households are better planners than others, and therefore they get richer harvests. But everyone must plan to some degree to get any harvest. Above all, a person must not forget his commitments. He will not be allowed to forget his debts, and he must remember his credits to survive.

When, therefore, the Land Dayak works for others, if they are outside the limits of his household, he does so purely as a business transaction in which the coin is labour. The system works smoothly. But it does so only because everybody holds the coin at its proper value, not as something to be given away but as a counter in a fair exchange based upon respect for contract. The fact that all book-keeping is done in the head must make this concept of labour a most dominant one in people's minds. It would therefore be very disturbing to do work for others without recompense. If the idea that one did so were to spread, one would soon find oneself without a bite to eat, or without a roof over one's head, because the same system holds of all work, and work of one kind is interchangeable with another.

Is there any need to wonder further why the Dayak takes a moral exception to working for the public when some of the public fails to appear? He feels as would a European who had his income-tax doubled to make up for a neighbour who said he did not want to pay.

As to why some of the people do not turn up to clean the village, the reason is simple enough. The idea does not appeal. The tone of the meeting would have told them that it does not appeal much to anyone. They need fear little more than a crocodile condemnation, probably cloaking relief on the part of those who did turn up that they too will now have to waste time on something which they feel is rather silly.

And from their point of view it is rather silly. While they live in longhouses twenty feet above the ground, refuse must be tipped overboard. If it is going overboard, pigs should be there to eat it. If there are pigs, there is going to be a general mess. In any case, everyone likes the mess. It is better than the growth covering most of the rest of the world, in which mosquitoes would breed. The people should like to please the District Officer—but, in the meantime, to reach the longhouse we shall just have to make our way through the mess, hoping there is a duck-walk if it has been raining heavily.

IV

THE LONGHOUSE

A DUCK-WALK is not a great help to the drunk. If the visitor is being given a full traditional village welcome, he will certainly be drunk by the time he reaches the steps leading up to the first of the two longhouses at Mentu Tapuh, even though they are only two hundred yards from the landing-stage. It is true that usually only a most distinguished visitor, such as a Governor, can hope for such a welcome —and even he may miss out if the people fear him too grand to brook the woman-handling which it involves. An ordinary visitor must resign himself to a reception not much less warm but a lot less expensive. Luckily I became extraordinary after three months' stay had proved me not to be a bird of passage like every past pallid-skinned visitor. Then the people, in their kindness, decided to extend me a full welcome. With Grandfather Ichau as good company I was shooed out of the village one afternoon to sleep the night in a hut a mile or two downstream. In the morning we were to re-enter the village in triumph, like Kichapi returning from the wars.

The high moment of the ceremony was to be firing of brass cannon over our canoe. Many Dayak villages have a few such cannon. They are of ancient Malay origin, and are greatly treasured. Mentu Tapuh had three. Now it has one, and it is this reduction in number, and not the importance of the visitor, which will make the day of the welcome long remembered. The Dayaks love a bang. Persons who own muzzle-loading shotguns, which look suicidal and sound as though the suicide is done, are allowed by the Government to buy a small ration of gunpowder each month. It is usually carefully conserved for hunting. But on this occasion the prospect of an extraordinary bang lured them into putting all their month's rations into the two cannon. The bang was shattering. It shattered both cannon to pieces. No one was hurt. The ancestors hovering around, to partake of the offerings and watch the fun, must have diverted the flying brass on to their own invulnerable presences. Later there were to be disputes about who should pay for the cannon. Some persons suggested that, as I was the one being honoured, it should be me. But such debates belonged to another day. For the present it was enough that the day had begun with a bang such as never had come from the cannon before, nor ever would again.

Before our canoe neared the shore, out waded the girls. Below their waists they wore their brightest sarongs, preserved for gala days, clasped, in the case of girls fortunate enough to have them, with precious heirloom belts made of linked Mexican or Chinese dollars, or of silver strips. From waist to shoulder each girl had only a scarlet scarf passing between her breasts. Every girl carried a bottle of wine— wine brewed from a grain known to us as Job's tears, an odd name for a grain so consoling. It may be planted only by old men, but at Mentu Tapuh they have a kind thought for all, young and old, and there is plenty of the consequence to go round at festival times. No harm comes. No one gets really drunk, because everyone likes to stay sober enough to drink some more. The wine is milky, sweet and strong. The aim of every girl, nearly half a hundred of them, was to force some of her wine down our throats. They were single-minded and successful. By the time we reached the steps up to the longhouse the day had taken on a new complexion.

A popular Dayak song begins, 'We love to see the stranger coming here, coming up the steps, stepping on the top step, and having it break down.' The steps consist of a notched tree-trunk, not usually hard for a European to negotiate, and only occasionally collapsing under his greater weight. But on this especial morning the help the girls competed to give certainly got us more safely to the top and across the rather shaky outer platform on to the firm inner verandah, where the old men were waiting near the offerings, the essence of which was to go to the gods, and to which they were quite welcome because the substance was to go to us and to our entertainers. We were now in the Dayak home. Had it been our first visit, I am sure the sight would have surprised us into sobriety.

A Dayak longhouse looks just like what its name implies—a long house. At Mentu Tapuh there are two longhouses and one is very long —over two hundred yards. It is about twenty yards wide. The whole structure is raised about sixteen feet off the ground on hardwood piles, and is roofed over in part by sago-palm leaf and in part by hardwood shingles. Two hundred and fifty people live in it. The inside is even more impressive than the outside. Two verandahs run along its entire length, the outer one an uncovered platform used mainly for drying paddy in the sun, and the inner one, beneath the roof, serving as a work-place for the women to pound their paddy into rice, as a social meeting-place, and as a passage-way off which open doors into the rear half of the longhouse, which is so divided as to form a series of living rooms. The general effect of the building is to suggest a pattern of living at the very opposite remove from our own individualistic system.

Indeed, if unfortunately—most unfortunately—Mentu Tapuh were to be buried under the silt of an extra large flood, and a thousand years later an archaeologist of the London school were to dig it up, he would probably conclude that here dwelt a people with a highly communal, if not communistic, mode of life. Clearly they shared a common dwelling with a minimum of family separation in small rooms at the rear. To build such a massive structure they must have had a well-organized social system, probably a system of clans under strong chiefs. Without the records of social anthropologists to guide them—these records even more unfortunately having been lost also in the flood—there is scarcely a limit to the conclusions which might be drawn. There would be nothing wrong with these conclusions except that they would be false. For the fact of the matter is that a Dayak longhouse is not a long house. It only looks like one. It is in reality a series of houses separately built but joined together. The mode of Dayak life, far from being the very opposite of our own, is in some ways its apotheosis.

We can get a better idea of what a longhouse is if we imagine first a terrace of houses in a London street, and then imagine both the houses and the street together raised on piles, and the eaves of the houses so sloped and extended as to cover most of the street. There is one important difference. The London street is publicly owned. Its equivalent, the longhouse verandah, is not so owned. The households whose living rooms open on to the verandah each own that portion of it which extends along the front of their room. They build it, and they are responsible for its upkeep. Once one becomes aware of this fact of individual ownership, a number of things about the longhouse become clearer. The variation in its condition is explained. Although it is in every household's interest to keep its verandah in good repair, a busy man, or a lazy man, may neglect to do so. For this reason, a visitor should bear carefully in mind the fact that the part of the verandah on which he is being entertained will be the most respectable part, so that when, during a lull in the honours being paid to him, he goes on to explore the remainder he will take care not to walk with too proud a step.

We can also now offer an explanation for the sometime state of the steps, alluded to in the song. They may, be steps which a man has put down in front of his own section of the verandah to give himself and his family quicker access to the ground. He may not be a lazy man. He may maintain his part of the verandah very well, for he will reason that although his neighbours use it to get along to other parts of the longhouse he uses their portions equally for the same purpose. But the steps are different. He alone puts them down. Other persons use them. He gets nothing in return. Therefore he may decline, quite rightly, to make them fit for general traffic, or to bother to replace them immediately he notices their weakening. He is not mean. Everyone is welcome to use them at their peril. I am not suggesting that there are no good steps—some are put up by co-operative endeavour—but merely that it is wise to be circumspect. Now, in fairness, we must express our conviction, and certainly our hope, that the archaeologist would give the right weight to these variations in the condition of the longhouse, and would not in fact take the wrong steps.

Why the Land Dayaks, and the other peoples in South East Asia who have similar types of dwellings, should have chosen to build in this fashion can only be guessed at. It may have been for defence. Up from the ground, and all together, the villagers would have been protected against surprise. Head-hunting raids seem often to have been sneak attacks against the unwary. The greatest danger a long-house faced must have been fire. There is at any time a considerable risk of longhouses catching alight. The upper longhouse at Mentu Tapuh disappeared in a blaze the year before I arrived, and was fully rebuilt only just before I left. There is no need to bother trying to put such a fire out. All that the residents can profitably do is enjoy the spectacle and take comfort in the thought that it will be memorable. Nevertheless such fires are more readily started by the persons in a longhouse, careless about their family hearths, than they would be by visitors calling for their heads. Hardwood piles are not easily set alight. An enemy's chance of roasting the residents must have involved an almost equal chance to him of being boiled in water poured between the slats comprising the longhouse floor.

There are good reasons why the people continue to live in longhouses. One reason is purely economical. To build attached houses saves material. This is quite important to the Dayaks, because on the whole their longhouses are well-built, with framework and interior walls of timber laboriously hand-sawn in the jungle. Even when one can use the neighbour's wall, subject perhaps to one's supplying half of it, it may require all the time one can spare from food-getting for two or three years to amass the material for a house. It can usually be done in this time, too, only when a man has a wife who can free him for the work through her own work in the fields.

The wife's help does not go unrecognized. A man whom we shall keep nameless since he was—at all other times—a gentleman whom we do not wish to libel, had just completed a new house. It was much the finest one in the longhouse, and indeed in the whole village. Pride may have led him to contemplate a new wife to go along with it. Certainly a domestic quarrel broke out. It began when his existing wife, of many wrinkle-bringing years, was cooking rice for the evening meal on the brand-new fireplace. She left the pot for a while, and returned to find her husband's hunting dog finishing up the contents. She kicked the dog so hard that her husband claimed she nearly slew it. He swore at her. He swore at her inside the house. Then he swore at her outside. He swore so hard that all the village heard, and heard with relish for such performances enliven the evening air but seldom. It was more than blind rage which led the husband to swear outside as well as inside. He wished to oblige his wife, in order to clear herself from shame, to take action against him. He could then counter her complaints with allegations enormous enough to win him public approval for a divorce.

To a point, his scheme was successful. The wife hurried to Grandfather Ichau, the village headman, who called a meeting for the next day to consider the case. Anyone could have come along to this meeting but matters of this kind are usually left to a few old men and the disputing parties. The court was informal, smoking, the chewing of betel, and the relaxation of incidental gossip being recognized as aids to sound judgment. After a whole morning of consideration, a decision was reached, and Grandfather Ichau summed it up. The wife was wrong, he said, to kick the dog so hard as to endanger its future usefulness to her husband. She was so wrong that her husband need pay no compensation to her for the insults. But she was not so wrong as to justify her husband's evicting her from the new home. If her husband wished to part from her, he must be the one to go away from the house, for her work had helped to build it as much as his. This meant that the husband could have either his new house or his new wife, but not both. He preferred the house, and he, wife and dog were well settled into it when I had unhappily to leave Mentu Tapuh.

The chief value to the people of their longhouse form of dwelling is not, however, to be found in ease of building. Longhouse living is part of the whole mode of social life. The particular ways in which the people do their work and have their fun are helped by it.

In the longhouse the people are together. They are a very close neighbourhood, always on one another's doorsteps, constantly mingling by chance, and finding it simple to meet one another, or join all together, purposely. They need not be a formally organized community because they are a community by situation—a crowd united by common interests, by belief in a common fate, by mutual need, and by many diverse ties of blood and friendship and debt and credit. The Land Dayaks have solved a great human problem—how to be independent and yet never be isolated. It is no wonder that none of them commits suicide. I could not discover a single case of that having happened. One woman did make a threat to do so, but its calculated effect was to mobilize plenty of restrainers. In the longhouse it is possible to be an individualist and yet lead a cosy life of company. If one is shamed or angry, one can sulk and yet never be forgotten.

The many neighbours easy to meet also makes smoother the system of labour by agreement. Persons can make up their own minds with whom they will work because there are plenty of people close at hand from whom to pick and choose. They do pick and choose a great deal, thus enjoying variety of companionship and work-place. This variety helps to unite the villagers in a common fellowship and gives them all a personal attachment to the whole village territory, which they will jointly defend against outsiders, even though each villager has rights over only a part of it.

The sense of community also receives a great but subtle strengthening through bonds of blood between villagers. Many societies in the world organize much of their social and economic life according to a regular system of rights and obligations defined by blood relationships. Not

---

PLATE I

The mountain at Mentu Tapuh seen from the verandah of the upper longhouse. On the right is part of the headhouse and, in the centre, the writer's house. The low building is a fowl-house.

only is such a system unnecessary for the Land Dayaks in view of their alternative system of free choice of work-mates and play-mates, it is also impractical for them, because members of a village may be diversely related, or sometimes barely related at all, to their fellow-villagers. Some may be husbands newly arrived in the village, others may be wives also newly come; some may be descendants of the first pioneers, others of later settlers, perhaps of different ancestral origin. Land Dayak society is free and open. Anyone may marry into it, or be admitted through the charity or goodwill of those already there. Stress on particular relationships, as necessarily better or more binding than others of a different kind, is out of place in this jungle democracy. It could only divide, when the need is to unite. For these reasons, kinship relationships beyond the family are for the Land Dayaks a personal and not a social matter. But as such they play an important part in keeping the society together.

The people are concerned with their close relatives, and then generally only with those who live near at hand. Remote ancestral connections are not much remembered. Almost as few Dayaks as Europeans know the identity of their great-grandparents, and some do not even know that of grandparents belonging to a different village. It is not that the Dayaks fear to look down their family trees, as many of us might, for they do not believe that children are stained by the sins of their forebears. The supreme deity creates each new soul, and if he likes to put it into a body ill-conceived, that is his business. The new life is god-given equally with any other. Shame may be a stronger sanction with the Land Dayaks than with us, but it is usually short-lived, and in the extreme is never more than a life-sentence. The reason that the Dayaks do not usually look far down their family trees is simply that they do not often see much purpose in doing so. With any people, genealogies are mainly of concern only to those who have a vested interest in them.

Actually Land Dayaks do have a vested interest in them, but it is not one which demands much attention. Rights to land descend from the ancestor, sometimes several generations back, who first

---

PLATE II

The steps up to the longhouse. The smaller buildings on right and left are shelters for the drying of paddy before its removal to the main stores on the outskirts of the village. The roofs of the shelters can be opened to let in the sun and the piles are protected by rat guards.

E

farmed it. But it is enough for the ordinary person to know that the land was farmed by his father, or by almost any other relative, since children of both sexes inherit land equally. Presumably his father's claim was good: so his must be good too.

There are in most villages one or two old men who are reputed to know enough about genealogies to settle the rare disputes about land which arise between persons in the same village. The public is content to leave the authority to them, which enables them to exercise it in accordance with expediency as well as historic fact. Indeed the forgetting of ancestral connections has the valuable effect of keeping land ownership more or less in tune with need, because families which do not make use of some of the areas to which they are entitled may fail to pass on their rights to their descendants.

There is some danger of our overlooking the part which poor memory, and other human weaknesses, play in society. In describing a social system, an anthropologist must, if his work is to be anything less than an encyclopaedia, abstract its most general features, but he would fall into a grievous error if he concluded that his generalizations were necessarily principles of action for the people concerned. A society is not an organism. It is a lot of people with imperfect memories and different wills always striving to suit their traditional and present circumstances to themselves. Being illiterate, one of the circumstances the Land Dayaks do not yet have to put up with is the existence of written records. Unconsciously they can remake their history to suit their situation—or consciously if they have to make out a case before a Government court in a land dispute with another village.

Attention to genealogies would seem to be needed for the ancestral cult, which is the main part of Land Dayak religion. It is not needed. The ancestors called upon may be anyone's ancestors. In fact they include everyone's ancestors, for the first call the priest makes is to the 'mothers and fathers of all the people here'. Although this invitation is meant to embrace forebears of any generation, it is the true parents whom the priest has most in mind, for he goes on to speak particularly of the mothers, in terms of his own mother, saying: 'Spirit of my mother! Who chewed in your mouth the food to give me height and size, to make me healthy, tall, well-formed and fat; to make me able to bite, to utter, to speak, to laugh, to carry a knife at my side and a fine basket with materials for betel-chewing; to make me able to go into the jungle and able to come out again.' Since this first call is issued to all ancestors anonymously, even a person unlucky enough not to be quite sure who his immediate ancestors were could feel nevertheless that they were included, and he could therefore expect the same blessings from them as anyone else from their ancestors.

After making the general call, the priest proceeds to list a number of the more ancient dead by name. These dead are not thought of in terms of their blood relationship to the living, which may be quite unknown. They are simply men, and occasionally women, famed in their day for their rich paddy harvests, their wealth, their wisdom, their leadership, their skill as priests, or as the possessors of any other desirable qualities which the present generation would like to acquire from them. They are everybody's patron spirits, and because this is so the ancestral cult, instead of stressing genealogical distinctions, serves to unify villagers who may in fact be of very different ancestral stocks.

The emphasis in relationships is in fact placed on the rising genera-tion rather than on the past. As soon as a child is born to a married couple, the husband calls his wife 'the mother of the infant', and she calls him 'the father of the infant'. There is nothing very odd about this: not so far. It is simply that parents in Dayak society are always, instead of as in English society very often, 'Mum' and 'Dad' to the whole family circle. But the Dayak system is carried much further. The terms 'father', or 'mother', 'of the infant' are fitting only while the infant remains an infant, and they can be safely used only by the legitimate companions in its procreation. For more general use terms less anonymous are needed. These are got by each person, when he or she has been a parent for a year or two, or when an age has been reached at which parenthood would have been normal, electing to become known as the 'father' or 'mother' of some particular named child.

This usage is a little odd, certainly. But it is still not outstandingly odd. It is common enough in the world for the term 'teknonymy' to have been coined for it. Its worst feature is that it turns our correct European usage upside down. We take our names—our surnames—from our parents. The Dayak parents take their names from their children. By doing so, they are behaving inconveniently, to say the very least. However, the Government is doing its best to make them see the light. For instance, when a Dayak applies for a licence to have a gun, he is asked bluntly to state his name. He cannot answer without embarrassment, for the best Dayak form forbids a man to speak his own name. Someone else should supply it if necessary. The next question, 'What is your father's name?' is worse still. Children should

not use the personal names of their parents, and if their parents happen
to be dead it is actually dangerous for them to do so. We cannot
fairly blame the Government, since uniformity is its instrument.
Furthermore, the Dayaks are not quite at a loss under the new system.
I know one man who got licences for five guns despite all the Government's devices to ensure that he got no more than one.

Incorrect though the Dayak naming system is, there is nothing
unique about it as so far described. But the Dayaks are an individual
as well as an individualistic people. They might be said to have their
own 'genius', and in this case it gives their teknonymy a quite unusual
feature. The child whose name is taken need not be an actual child of
the taker of its name. It need not be a relative. It is usually a human
being, but even this is not always so. Sometimes it seemed to me
as if the Land Dayaks had deliberately studied the generalizations of
anthropology in order to break them. One man in Mentu Tapuh was
known as 'Father of Mangai', and it turned out that Mangai was a
favourite hunting dog. An old woman was known as 'Grandmother
of Badad', Badad being a cat. This reminds me of a feature of the
Dayak system not yet mentioned. It is that as a person moves on in
age, he passes into a grandparent grade, and, taking the name of a
child of a generation lower than that of the first child, to whom the
the second child is not necessarily related, he or she becomes the
'grandfather' or 'grandmother' of that child.

The cases involving the cat and the dog are anomalous cases, created
to confound anthropologists. Anomalous too was the name given to
me. Here the children displayed a striking little bit of their 'genius'. In
order to distinguish me from other 'grandfathers' in the village,
they adopted the term *babeh*, which is a dialectical variation, current
across the border, of *babuk*, their own term for 'grandfather'. Translated literally this name meant 'the old creature from Dutch Borneo',
although the children knew very well that I did not come from
there. I say 'creature' rather than 'old man' because the children's
estimation of me was supplemented by a considered adult statement.
A man remarked to me one day that he should like to build a house
next to mine, which lay almost across the path from the longhouses
to the river—a most convenient situation for watching everyone's
coming and going on their own business. I said, 'Why don't you?'
'This place is the haunt of a demon,' he replied, 'and if I build here, my
family will fall sick', and he quoted the case of a man who had lived
there and who had fallen grievously sick. 'But I've lived here,' I said,

'and I've not fallen sick.' 'Yes,' he said, 'but that's natural enough. Demons won't hurt their own kind!'

Much more typical of the naming system is the case of the man whose personal name is Bawut. He was given this name by his parents after his first year or so during which time he had been known simply as *suweh*, or 'infant'. He grew up through the *baduput*, or 'little boy', stage and the *bujang*, or 'young man' stage, until, coming to the age at which most men are married, he reached the *amang*, or 'father', stage. At this stage of life personal names go out of use, as do our Christian names, except between close friends of one's own age or by older relatives speaking to younger. What, therefore, was Bawut to be called in future? His own children could call him 'my' or 'our' father. But for general use he needed a name as definite as his old one. To get it he adopted the name of a fairly distantly related child in the generation below his own, and became known as Amang Mali, or 'Father (of) Mali'. The passing years brought him to the next stage, the final one short of the after-world, which we hope will not need his presence for many, many more years yet. He now became a 'grandfather'. Once more he required a new name for general use. He selected a child from amongst the present brood in the village, and adopted its name. And so the kindly, wise, shrewd, gentle-spoken old man, who had begun life as Bawut, became Babuk Ichau, or 'Grandfather (of) Ichau'.

The system is a good one, linking generation to generation in a way which suggests at once the respect of the young for the old and the solicitude of the old for the young. The solicitude is almost always there. The respect is not obliged, for in this democracy the young are free as well as the adults, but the respect is generally freely yielded. Since everyone is figuratively either a child, a parent, or a grandparent, the effect of the system is to unite the village symbolically into one great family.

There is no especial tie to the child whose name is taken. If it is not one's own child or grandchild, it is thought to be a kind gesture to leave it, when one dies, some small token to show that it has been brought symbolically within the family. But no one mistakes a symbolic relationship for a real one, no more than an Englishman mistakes his God-children for his own children. The relatives who count for the Land Dayaks are their real, close relatives—the families into which they were born, the families which they create, and the immediate connections of these two families. Their attitudes are indeed very

closely similar to our own. They classify their relatives in almost
the same way. They may marry any one who is not closer than a
second cousin and who is of the opposite sex. They have no ban on
the deceased wife's sister. Kichapi, the hero of our Story, did not
even recognize a ban on his undeceased wife's sister. They place a little
greater value than we do, however, on relationships to parents-in-law
and brothers- and sisters-in-law. This has the useful effect of enabling
people who join the village upon marriage to feel quickly at home.

The emphasis upon close relationships through marriage and through
children serves the needs of the society well. It means that sentimental
attachments due to kinship are constantly being modified in a way
which keeps them in line with the most important actual relationships of the people, so that the families-in-being form the links in a
network of ties which extends over the village. It is a changing network of no very clear pattern. It is formed of more weak strands than
strong, for intimacies are not confined to kinship and they do not
even always accompany it. Each person, too, is aware mainly of the
strands radiating from himself, and about some of these he does not
bother. But, looked at for the village as a whole, the network can be
seen to be a human arrangement like an electric grid, constantly fed
by small charges of emotions. It is crossed by other grids of companionship, and of relationships of work and play. The force in the complex
whole creates the community and keeps it alive.

The Land Dayak village community can best be understood as a
kind of club—with rules, and occasional subscriptions in the form of
contributions to festivals, but with no entrance bar according to birth,
although birth automatically qualifies. It is a club which means a
great deal to all who are in it. They can find work-mates and companions among their fellow-members, they can enjoy the club facilities
—the headhouse, the bathing-place, and all the village confines—
they can share in its festivals, and they can count on it for alliance
against the threats of a most dangerous world.

But it can work well as a club only if all its members can share
in it equally. There is no room for cliques, because they would leave
some persons out in the cold. Divisions can be permitted only if they
are of a kind which will give each person a place in one of them.
Household divisions alone can do so. The households are, therefore,
the only definite groupings within the Dayak village. They leave
no one out in the cold, although some persons have a warmer or
wider domestic circle than others.

V

THE HOUSEHOLD

THE Land Dayaks, like the rest of mankind, live in households for reasons simple enough for any sociologist to state in a few words. Their individualism, which makes them so unlike a herd, obviously cannot go so far as to make them hermits. They must provide for themselves shelter and comfort, gain their food, cook it, and rear offspring. None of these things would they care to do alone, and alone they certainly could not do them all.

The make-up of these households is very much like that of households in our own society. Each household begins with a family of parents and children. It endures by one of the children, but ideally only one, forming his own family within its fold. The process continues in each generation. The household is thus a living stem of the family tree. In each generation, if other children than the one marry, they branch out to form households of their own, or else are absorbed as husbands or wives into different households. The process is much the same as that which perpetuates the ancestral homes of England—in slum or castle, but more rarely in suburbia where parents often wither alone.

The process is not quite the same in the English castle and in the Dayak home in the longhouse. In the first place, the English elevate sons above daughters. In the Dayak democracy sons and daughters are equal. It may be a wife or it may be a husband who is taken into the household to keep it going. Secondly, in the castle it is the eldest child who has the best right to stay. In the room in the longhouse it is the youngest child. Once again, the Dayaks are quite brazen about their reversal of the proper order of things. They say that the older children have a longer time in which to prepare to set up for themselves, and also that in his youth the youngest child has to work with more aged parents. Therefore they favour this child. They single it out by a special term. It has first place in their interest. Europeans expect the most of their first-born. The Dayaks expect it of their last-born. It is not at all strange, therefore, that in our Story, the most famous story of the Dayak homeland, Kichapi, the hero, should be the youngest child of his family, that he should out-top and lead all his brothers.

We may note one other thing about Kichapi. The Land Dayaks are monogamous. They are so in fact at least, although it is the first wife and not a religious principle which upholds the fact. But Kichapi married two wives. This apparent contradition between fiction and fact admits of a very simple explanation. The authors of the Story, long ago, were concerned to show Kichapi as in all ways bold.

Sometimes the membership of a Dayak household ranges from great-grandparents to great-grandchildren, but usually the range is shorter, from one grandparent to a few grandchildren with perhaps an odd relative or two who has never formed a home or whose home has gone, all maintaining themselves in a close-knit fellowship against the many mischances which ever threaten to shorten the range further. The household group is rarely large. Many children die. Few persons receive the blessing of long old age which the priest seeks from the ancestors at the end of every invocation. In Mentu Tapuh the average number of persons in a household was six.

The household may be thought of as a company almost in the business sense. It has its capital in house, fields, tools and weapons. The yield from harvest, gathering and hunting forms a common income, and the right of members to draw upon it for their personal wants is governed to some degree by the amount they have contributed to it. Everyone old enough to do so should make some contribution to the household's food, or at least do something for its general welfare, to compensate for the amount he eats.

There is not usually much surplus over food requirements. Sometimes there is none. Sometimes there is less than none, either because of a bad harvest or because too much of the harvest has had to be sold to buy clothing. In either case, the dying months of the year are hard times. The people must keep themselves alive on wild sago, or on edible fern fronds, bamboo shoots, or leaves, which instead of serving as a relish for rice now serve as its substitute. Only the very young children are spared the pinch. Enough rice is usually saved, or borrowed, for them. They need it, for the Dayak baby, on the very day of its birth, is started on rice, masticated first by its mother and taken along with her milk.

In most years, however, most households do contrive to make a certain quantity of paddy available for purposes other than food. It is in the expending of this quantity that some balance comes about between amount of work and amount of reward. It is a very rough balance, and it results more from circumstance than from recognition of rights. But the expectation of it encourages workers, or at least helps to reconcile them to the harder tasks. The balance can be seen in the case of the young women. They do the hardest work of all. They work at least as hard in the fields as the young men. In addition they have domestic tasks. For instance, they must carry up from the river the household's water supply. This is heavy work, for the bamboo containers to be filled are many; but it is not man's work. Shame alone would deter a man from it. For a while in Mentu Tapuh a man used to pass my house each night loaded with containers. His wife had left him. He had to carry his own water. So he sneaked down to get it in the dark. It is some compensation for the harder work of the young women that the largest share of personal expenditure on the household budget tends to go to them, in the way of sarongs and articles of adornment.

The same position holds with the children. Little boys lead a lazy life. Little girls work, feeding the fowls, shutting them up in their baskets—one fowl to a basket—each night, letting them out each morning, feeding the pigs, drying paddy in the sun and helping to pound it. But little boys have very little clothing, while little girls have a little more, with some bright paste-jewellery, and lipstick on gala days, to go along with it. On the other hand, little boys have bigger appetites, and this brings us to a truth which, in justice to the women and the little girls, we must not overlook. It is that the extra share they get on the budget is not proportional to their extra work. This is not because the Land Dayak men wish to be unfair to their women; nor are they lazy. It is necessity which presses, and the women recognize it well.

In Land Dayak society men live longer than women. The reason is that women do more work. In our society women live longer than men.

Sometimes there is a real budget surplus. In the most fortunate cases, the happy farmer, when a bumper new harvest is to be stored, may look into the bins in his granary to find them still half full. Several enchanting possibilities then open before him. He may sell the surplus to a Chinese trader, and spend the money quickly—on a trip to the bazaar, salt fish for the family, a wardrobe—there is no need to list all the ways of evaporating wealth. A second possibility is also to sell the surplus, but to save the cash. This is not a bad way of dealing with the situation. Money can breed money. Grandfather Ichau, who was always a successful farmer, because he used good magic to back up his good sense, took this way with some of his surplus. He kept his money holdings secret, for he had no wish to be thought a miser. The secret was revealed by the misfortune to my boat already alluded to. Apparently he carried most of his money, in the form of notes, on his person when he went away from the village. As soon as he reached the bank, after the misfortune in mid-river, his first concern was to spread the notes around him to dry. He looked a venerable figure as he sat in the sun, a dripping Croesus in a sea of Sarawak dollars.

But this way of dealing with the surplus, never well-established, is now under a cloud, as a result of the war and its aftermath. It is alleged that one Japanese officer used to pay Dayak conscripted workers at Serian by bringing along a hand-press to run off dollars as they were needed. Whether this particular story is true or not, the complete loss of value of Japanese money and the inflation of the liberated Sarawak and Malayan dollars have seriously undermined faith in the currency. The Land Dayaks have so little money that they are greatly impressed by what happens to it. And they do not like what has happened lately. Nyandoh told me that his father was nowadays constantly impressing on him and his brother the maxim: 'Save paddy. Paddy doesn't devaluate.'

This is good advice up to a point, a point few households have the luck to pass. A reserve stock of paddy saves worry about a bad year. It may also bring a little harvest of its own through loans to needy neighbours. But the investment market is really poor. It is ruined by the investors themselves, who are almost as exorbitant as Shylock. Or should we say as public-spirited as Shylock, for how could a man who asked for a pound of flesh be said to encourage borrowing? The Dayak terms are less severe but they are still painful enough to keep most people out of debt. The usual rate of interest is 50% or 75% for the duration of the loan, which should be only until the next harvest. Grandfather Ichau has recently raised his rate to 100%—every gallon of paddy borrowed should be repaid by two gallons. The reason he gives for charging more than other lenders is logical. Having the largest stocks, he has to loan more. Therefore it is right that he should get more back.

The point at which the saving of paddy becomes impractical is the point at which it begins to go bad. Stocks can safely be kept for only three years or so, after which they must be disposed of to a Chinese trader as 'fresh stock' as quickly as possible. Before, or when this point is reached, the surplus may be converted into other forms of wealth, which can provide a consolidated fund for the household. Because of their traditional worth, the most valued objects are Chinese earthenware jars, brass cannon, and brass gongs. Of lower value are plates and small bowls. Such articles are a true investment because, everyone reckoning them at a standard value—a value which has hardly altered for at least fifty years—they can be exchanged for food or for anything else should hard times fall upon their owners. The jars and cannon and gongs are therefore to the Dayaks as gold, and the plates and bowls as silver—visible, durable and precious.

But they are not only as gold and silver. They are also as precious stones. The Dayak—a connoisseur—loves them for their beauty. More importantly, they are not tokens, but absolute wealth. A Dayak will not part with his jars lightly. Those he presents to his gods, or, more rarely, those which are placed beside the grave of an honoured kinsman, are usually damaged, because fortunately spirits, being other-worldly, prefer broken articles. If a household has no broken jars, the honoured kinsman usually goes without. The gods and the demons are luckier because the same articles can be presented to them over and over again. Only very reluctantly will a household exchange its jars or other such articles. Instead it does its best to seek and to keep them, for every household wants to be wealthy.

Kichapi boasts that his friend the Dragon-chief is 'wealthy in Javanese gongs, rich in the jars called *tajau lingka*'. It is unlikely that Kichapi was a snob. A household is proud of its jars. It is pleased to be able to send a gong to be hung in the festival orchestra. It enjoys being able to hold its own special festivals not only because of the supernatural benefits which these festivals bring and because of the fun of them, but also because they advertise the fact that the household has the wherewithal to stage them. When they are over, pieces of plant of some kind are hung above the door of the house as a sign to the demons, but visible to everyone, that a festival of that particular type has been held. Still, there is very little ostentation. The jars in a household are rarely placed under a visitor's nose. The gongs sent to the orchestra are not labelled. The pieces of plant soon wither.

There is little ostentation because Dayak ideology provides it with little purpose. Constant show is gratifying if it can make other people uncomfortable. It cannot make Dayaks uncomfortable, because the final condition of success or failure is the favour of fortune, variously conceived. The poor consider their poverty the result of circumstances which have made effort fruitless; the lazy of circumstances which would make it futile. Compared to our own capitalism, Dayak capitalism may be less charitable in deed. A Dayak need have no moral qualms about holding on to what he gets. But Dayak capitalism is more charitable in thought, because it looks more tolerantly upon fellow-men who fail. Let us hasten to say that these statements are not wholly true. Since the Dayaks are human—and thus both kind and cruel—ideology can only partly mould their behaviour. But there is a lot of truth in a half-truth, and it is rather more than a half-truth to say that in Dayak society the rich are respected but the poor are not despised.

Wealth does bring respect. The kind of respect may depend upon the reason for the wealth. Kichapi spoke of the wealth of his friend the Dragon-chief to prove the power of the medicines which he had stolen from him. He hoped to frighten his enemies. But usually the reasons for the wealth are not thought about clearly. It is enough that the rich are proven successes. Success is admired because it represents something everyone would like to achieve. The rich man can therefore hope to stand first among equals in the minds of other men, and he may even stand first among equals in practical dealings with them, for, if any voluntary following has perforce to be done, the rich are the best men to follow, because obviously they have a power above the ordinary. In fact the Government-appointed chiefs of Land Dayak districts are called *Orang Kaya*, meaning 'Rich Man'. This is not a traditional Dayak title—the words are not even Dayak, but Malay—but it is in tune with Dayak ideas. Grandfather Ichau had such a title, and enjoyed it, although continually declaring himself on the point of resigning it.

Today the jars, cannon and gongs are facing growing competition from newer items of appeal, such as shotguns, Coleman lanterns, and—as yet only in the dreams of the ambitious—outboard motors. This does not come from any change of mind in regard to wealth. The newer items are wanted because they are more useful. The Dayaks never spurned usefulness. They are not misers, and they are not strong traditionalists. When they invested in the jars, gongs and cannon, they did so because there was nothing else more useful available to them. The newer items are wealth just as much as the old, and wealth in this new form may be expected to confer almost as much general benefit as wealth in its older form. In some ways, perhaps, not quite as much, for the gods are greater traditionalists than men. Grandfather Ichau did present them his shotguns once or twice, but they are not generally thought, even by him, to have need of shotguns. Nor should they have need of Coleman lanterns in the after-world. If it were a gloomy after-world they might be glad of them, but in fact it is lit by a lovely celestial light. I remember clearly the first time I saw it. We were down by the landing-stage, a bunch of small boys and I, one most dark earthly day, when suddenly the trees across the river gleamed in light from a hidden sun. As we all looked with easier breaths, a little boy exclaimed, 'See, Grandfather! It's sunlight from *Sebayan*!'

In some ways, the benefit from the new form of wealth may actually be greater. Tuntong, the little boy who came from Suhu, remarked with great political sagacity one day, 'I see now what you really need to become an *Orang Kaya*. You need tea-cups and saucers, to entertain Europeans who come to the village.'

But although the changing form of wealth is not due to any new form of thinking, it may have new results. The older articles were more durable. They could be passed on down through the generations in a household, mellowing in human estimation with time, giving the household an enduring common interest and the children a prospect deriving from their fathers. The newer articles wear out. The children will have to earn them afresh, hindered rather than helped by the older members of their households. The change in the nature of wealth could therefore have a great effect on the community. But luckily it is not a matter we need bother about, for the change has barely begun. And it may not go far, because the Dayaks are poor, are likely to stay poor, and may unhappily get poorer.

VI

THE HEADHOUSE

THE room in the longhouse is the family home, where every member eats and keeps his few things, but it is not where every member sleeps. A common view in Borneo, no less than in other parts of the world, is that for the unpublic hours of the night, when lamps have been turned low and sleep is the only admitted aim, the unmarried of the two sexes should have a wall between them. Since the main Dayak family apartment is undivided, the separation requires either that the girls sleep outside the apartment or that the boys do so. The Sea Dayaks prefer the first alternative. The girls put themselves to bed in lofts built over the inner verandah in front of their family rooms. The Land Dayaks prefer the other alternative. In both cases the separation has the same effect. It is not made because the Dayak parents have any fear that their children may become incestuous. The separation of the two sexes has a more general social value. Because of it, marriage is made to stand out as the only proper state for cohabitation in the darkness. There are, of course, improper states.

The Sea Dayak girls go to their lofts and whether they are lonely there or not cannot be fairly stated, because there is only rumour to go on and rumour may well be false. Their loneliness should not in any case be great for they are close to their families, the loft being merely a second-storey extension of the house. The Land Dayak boys go further away—right outside the house—and go at an earlier age, but they are certainly never lonely. While they stay where they are · supposed to stay, they have the close companionship of others of their sex. Of this companionship they are fond, and the attraction of it is the main reason why boys like to sleep away from their family rooms at quite a young age.

Kichapi, the hero of our Story, began the practice on the very day of his birth. But he was exceptional. Eight or nine years is generally the earliest age at which boys leave the parental nest. After all, Kichapi spent seven years in the womb before he first came into the world.

There is no rule about the matter. The Dayaks indeed have little time for rules. Principles, they seem to feel, are for the weak-willed, and the average Dayak is about as weak-willed as the average cat. A boy might expect no more than a frown if he stayed on in the family home until he was forty. For occasional nights, or in exceptional circumstances, or if he is ailing, he need not fear even so much. It is when the family home in which he is found is not his own that the frown is more likely—and that is the home in which he is more likely to be found. Or at least more likely to be in, for to avoid the frown he should avoid being found.

The Land Dayak boys, so far as I know, never sleep in lofts. Kichapi, it is true, slept in one when he visited the longhouse of the Dragon-chief, but the most exciting thing about Kichapi was the novelty of what he did. The nearest to lofts that I have seen was at Suhu. There were a number of small raised huts built just off the outer edge of the outer platform of the longhouse, to which they were connected by short, precarious step-ways. Each one was shared by three or four men from neighbouring households. The huts looked like hen-houses, and the occupants had almost as little room as have Dayak hens in their baskets at night.

At Mentu Tapuh there was a more spacious arrangement. For much of the length of the inner verandah, along its outer edge, a platform about six feet wide and two feet high had been built close beneath the overhanging roof. Here at night in a long line lay the village unwedded—the unstirred but not unstirring young, the adolescents, the eligible, the rejected, and the retired; straight, curled or intertwined, bits of them caught in the half-light—a child's shoulder, delicately brown, an athletic patch of back, an emaciated calf, an outcropping of soles, gleaming white, new and old but none of them tender—the whole attenuated collection in a slightly restless sleep, testifying to its life by a low cacophony of snorts, snores, coughs and groans and grunts.

But neither of these arrangements, neither the bachelors' perches at Suhu nor the long counter-full of humanity at Mentu Tapuh, were normal. Both were the result of temporary circumstances—a long-lasting temporariness, but one which everybody in theory thought it proper to overcome as soon as possible. For there is a proper place for the unmarried male persons to sleep, and that proper place is the headhouse.

The headhouse is always the most elevated building in the village.

Sometimes, in villages of little spirit, it is built just off the outer edge of a longhouse verandah and only a little above it—in like position, indeed, to the Suhu bachelors' perches, but many times larger. But frequently the spot chosen for it is immediately above sharply sloping ground, so that the sensation one gets on first looking out from it is of a shockingly celestial suspension. For instance, in the village of Temong only eight or nine steps were needed to take one into the headhouse, yet when one crossed its expanse to the far side—it was magnificently wide—the nearest visible point of the globe was a stony stream bed at least a hundred and fifty feet below.

There are some villages which do not have the topography to create this kind of illusion, or which would spurn to do so. Mentu Tapuh was one of them. The headhouse there—the old headhouse which was in use when I first went to the village and where I was put to sleep with all the other un-mated or de-mated—was really very high. It was not connected to either longhouse. One mounted directly from the ground up a tree-trunk step-way, which elongated as one climbed.

Exactly how high and how big are such headhouses? No one seeking the truth of Dayak life should ask such a question. Measurements are purely physical comparisons, and purely physical comparisons are meaningless, because outlooks are different. I hope this is so, because I forgot actually to measure any of the headhouses. I should think that if a tape-measure had been applied to the headhouse at Mentu Tapuh it might have proved to be only about forty feet square and about thirty feet from floor-level to ground. But such a description would be of value only in a technological work, or for an architect's plan in case any reader wished to build a headhouse, which is unlikely. It provides no guide to opinion. The truth is that the Dayaks thought their headhouses very large and I thought them very high. Both our opinions were conditioned by experience.

The Dayak experience was the years-long labour of collecting all the material from the forest, of preparing it, and of putting it all together. The most vivid part of my experience came suddenly, at the village of Tasu. With two Dayak companions, I had come to the village—a phenomenon for the young and a rare spectacle for the rest. Everyone, perhaps two hundred or more men, women and

---

PLATE III

A Land Dayak maiden with her soul in a jar, a silver belt and a magical hat

children, crowded into the headhouse to see me. We were packed together, eager sardines well up in the sky, a loading far above the engineering specifications. There was no warning. A loud crack! A terrifying moment of descent! A split second of paralysis! Then a swaying as people scrambled out—the people nearest the door and furthest away from the visitors. Before the exodus was over an inspection had been made below. A main supporting pillar had snapped off a few feet above the ground, but the broken end had sunk in to form a new support. Reassured, the people began to crowd back. But the first of them coming in were passed by the visitors going out. Whereupon the longhouse verandah was made the new point of assembly.

Very, very occasionally headhouses do collapse. There was an unfortunate case in the village of Piching a few years ago. Sometimes, too, people fall from the longhouses. Two children fell while I was in Mentu Tapuh. The first was a girl who fell from the rafters, where she was stowing baskets, on to the floor, breaking her leg. The second was a boy who fell from the floor to the ground. He suffered very little injury, less than the boy who a few days later fell from a coconut palm. A sociologist, from his safer academic eminence, might be inclined to take a longer view past those who have actually felt the bump of a fall and say that such incidents have a 'function'. They gratify the people by reminding them of the high life they live.

The headhouse at Piching fell, and the one at Tasu nearly did, with us inside. Fortunately the people of Mentu Tapuh admitted their headhouse to be unsafe at a slightly earlier stage. I was glad when this admission was made, but glad also, in retrospect, that it had not been made sooner, before I had had a chance to know the headhouse, because of all the headhouses I saw this one was most like the one in which Kichapi was accommodated when he visited the village of his two loves.

In the headhouse in Gumiloh's village there was, at some immense height from the ground, a platform built below the floor proper. There was no such platform on the headhouse at Mentu Tapuh, but there could have been. At higher levels the houses were

---

PLATE IV

The longhouse verandah. The outer portion, which serves as a social centre, is floored with split bamboo. On the inner portion, floored with split areca palm trunks, women pound paddy outside the doors of their living rooms.

F

the same. There was first the main floor, and then above it a gallery—
an unusual feature in headhouses—extending outwards over the
floor for about eight feet from the walls. Up beyond the gallery the
walls sloped inwards very steeply to meet at a point below the stars.
The house was big by day, the smoke-blackened rafters giving a
greater age, and the spider-web curtains an ampler perspective, to the
roof. But if it was big by day, at night it vastly expanded, as the glow
from the hearth in the centre and from the wicks of a few unglassed
lamps made the corners remote and the roof an indefinite extension,
a barrier somewhere against the elements and the denizens of the sky
but unconfining to the spirits of its builders, or of their sons or grand-
sons. Brighter lights brought in for a village meeting might limit
the walls, showing up the sleeping mats rolled against them, but they
could scarcely reduce the roof. Coleman lanterns, now so much
sought, do, of course, threaten the mystery of this and other buildings,
but then they add a glitter to the Dayak night, and of the two forms
of romance the Dayaks prefer the brighter.

By definition a headhouse should be capitally adorned, and usually
this is so, although the adornments may fall below expectations.
Smoke-blackened like the rafters from which they hang, the heads
are usually inconspicuous. And their form is unexciting. A visitor
should not, however, expect too much. As in all major human pursuits,
so in head-preserving there is but a limited number of possibilities.
One is to dry the entire head—a troublesome process this, which
even in temperate New Zealand was developed on a large scale by the
Maoris only in response to the demands of the European market. A
preferable process begins with a separation of the head into its two
main divisions, the outer fleshy covering and the inner skull. Thereafter the process admits of three possible variations.

Theoretically both parts could be separately preserved, but this
possibility appears generally to be rejected out of a neatness of mind
which recognizes that the person of the slain is best represented by a
single remain. In practice, therefore, only two possibilities remain—
either to preserve the outer part, or to preserve the inner part. The
early Americans chose the outer part, the northerners with their
high-pressure temperament being satisfied with a roughly dried
scalp, while the more deliberate southerners, taking the complete
outer covering, carefully controlled the drying and moulded the
dwindling shape in its original likeness to produce the celebrated
shrunken but boneless 'heads' of Brazil.

The Maoris, then, preserved the whole head, and the Americans preserved the fleshy outer portion. The Dayaks, however, preserved the inner portion because, of the three practical possibilities, this was the most hygienic. As is made clear in the Story, the 'skinning' of the heads was a privilege granted usually to the most favoured village ladies but permanent value was attached only to the bony structure beneath. The visitor to the headhouse will not therefore be greeted by a line of whole heads each dangling by its long black hair but merely by a line of skulls suspended by strips of rattan or hung in baskets because the bone has begun to rot.

In a few cases there may not even be skulls, for heads are not essential to a headhouse, a seeming paradox explained by the fact that this name for the building is purely a European term not equivalent to the various Dayak terms, all of which can be translated as 'hall' or 'bachelors' residence'! All villages do wish to have heads and consider the headhouse the right repository for them, but they stand in much the same relationship to the true functions of the building as do antlers in a European hall, although the analogy is not otherwise close. The main importance of the heads was when they were first brought home. Once hung away in the headhouse little further active regard is paid to them.

This is so in the Mentu villages at least and I should have thought it so more generally were it not for an article in the London *News Chronicle* by a writer reporting on an evening spent in a Land Dayak village which he visited in the course of a tour sponsored by Unesco. Shortly after he and his companions on the tour arrived, the villagers invoked the spirit of a head to find out from 'the spirit of the mountain', of whom they lived in awe, whether or not the visitors could be received. Fortunately the answer was favourable.

Now there is no reason to doubt this interpretation of what happened and of the serious intent behind it. The writer in question did, certainly, have a keen eye for evidences of superstition. Seeing a bicycle hanging in the longhouse, he concluded that, since it was so far from a road, it must have a purely magical significance. Had he chanced to meet this bicycle on some blind corner of a jungle track, with its owner atop, it might have struck him as positively diabolical.

The Dayaks would, of course, wish to entertain the visitors from Unesco to the best of their resources. Still, there is nothing implausible in the account of the manner in which the head was employed. As yet the Dayaks have no Pope, although noble efforts are being made to bring them under the wing of one, and therefore they are unaware of the constraint of orthodoxy. Heads might be used in any variety of ways to suit local fancy. The fact remains that their main use, and the only one generally agreed upon, is that described in our Story. Once and once only, preferably when they are newly purloined from the slain, they may be presented as supreme offerings to the gods. Thereafter they are put in the headhouse to be left alone except perhaps for an occasional cleaning and a renewal of their bindings.

Hanging there, the heads have a very different meaning from the antlers in a British huntsman's hall. Sometimes the heads of treacherous jungle animals, especially the bear, are hung near them, and this suggests that they are looked upon as trophies. But the animal heads are not valued as are the human heads, and if they are given a place at all, it is less as proofs of prowess than as proofs of dangers overcome. The human heads are not trophies as we tend to think of trophies. They concern a much narrower and more desperate range of human endeavour.

Head-hunting was not, to any extent, a pursuit in its own right. In the main it was a result and not a cause of fighting between groups. The Land Dayak village-states were always liable to be attacked and sometimes they felt righteously provoked into attacking. In this situation it was a help to have some means of symbolizing the fighting need and fighting hope of the village, and the heads were collected for this purpose.

The heads were a choice among many possible symbols by means of which success in the past could be used to give confidence in the future. A strange choice it might seem to us, with our rougher battle techniques and vaster numbers of slain, but it was an adequate one for the Dayaks. Expressive of the personal combats which the little Dayak wars never got beyond, the heads were made into especially powerful symbols of village unity by being treated as the objects of grand village triumphs, and into symbols of supernatural support by their presentation to the gods. Their value would lessen as the victories, celebrations and ceremonies grew further off in time. But this did not result in urgent desire to seek replacements, for there were curbs on the fighting spirit.

Even without any other restraint, the value placed on heads itself actually tended to limit warfare. Presentation of the heads to the gods had to be made on pain of misfortune otherwise, but presentation, with its accompanying festivities, was costly in food and effort. There was little temptation, therefore, to collect heads randomly or often. As far as possible, fighting was restricted to prosperous times and times when the essential agriculture of the year was over, the Dayaks not having discovered our art of using war to create prosperity, that is to say, internal prosperity. They knew, of course, of the possibility of increasing prosperity by plunder. But there was usually only a faint chance of this for the balance of power within the Land Dayak world usually restricted head-collecting to small encounters which the losers would break off at the first loss to await an occasion more favourable to themselves.

It would be misleading to over-draw this picture of a world kept stable by cultural checks and balancing forces. Such pictures are very neat, and a credit to the sociologist who draws them, but the curse upon him is that they are constantly being upset by human wilfulness. They are based, too, upon statistical averages, and a statistical average cannot console a man, woman or young child decapitated irregularly, or restore a village utterly destroyed by circumstantial imbalance of power.

Also, and much worse for the Land Dayaks, they were not left alone within their own world. They were harassed by the Malays, and attacked by the Sea Dayaks, who, having gained the upper hand, were not restrained by a balance of power. In time a new balance of power may have come about, but it may not have included the Land Dayaks but merely operated in the area which they once occupied.

I refuse to believe that this would have happened. I believe the worthier people would have won in the end. The arrival of the Europeans was no doubt due to a recognition by Providence of the vastly superior worth of the Land Dayaks. There is also no doubt that, with all their worth, the Land Dayaks did live in a most dangerous world. The heads kept them aware of the fact. They were reminders of peril as well as sources of hope. The effect of the heads, over the years, was not therefore to encourage an active collecting zeal. The Land Dayaks are not wantonly bold. Their courage is of a quieter, unobjectionable kind. It is purely protective.

This was made clear to me one day during a discussion on the edibility of scaly ant-eater. A man remarked that it was no good to eat because it was a timid animal and he who ate it would become infected with its timidity. Nearly everyone laughed at this remark. Few of them put much weight on the theory that an animal's nature might be digested with its flesh. Village pig is the greatest delicacy of all. Most people are content to be governed by the taste of the flesh, unless they have some family taboo, and they knew that the taste of the scaly ant-eater was unattractive. But the speaker went on. 'Its eater will become so timid,' he said, 'that if he meets head-hunters in the countryside he will be too frightened to run away.' No one laughed at this additional remark except me. And I am ashamed of it, for the laughter came from the false bravado which is so easy when danger is remote.

The Land Dayaks do not pay much regard to courage as an abstract virtue. Even in our Story, where fancy could have been bold, there is little sign of such a rating of it. Where would the war-party have been without Kichapi, the hero? And even he owed his victories more to magic than to his own human heart. In the Story, too, all the battles are defensive except one, and that one was embarked upon with the aim of proving to the enemy that villagers could not be attacked, and their heads removed, with impunity.

The Land Dayaks do not pay much regard to courage as an abstract virtue because they know that necessity will probably be enough to draw forth all they have of it. Although they may appreciate such qualities when they are shown, they do not hold up valour and self-sacrifice as ideals. They believe that everyone has the right to do the best he can for himself. They have no harsh initiation rites to develop a Spartan youth. This does not mean that they are cowards. Let me hasten to say so, because I do not know whether they are or not. Thank goodness I never had to face head-hunters along with them to find out. Whether in other matters they are more or less hardy than Europeans it is difficult to say. In fact it would be ridiculous to try to say it, because both peoples are so varied amongst themselves.

Certainly the Land Dayaks were extremely varied, as I found out in the course of the little medical treatment I was able to give. One evening a young man persuaded me to make a deep exploration above his knee with a razor blade and a pair of forceps in search of a splinter which could at first be felt but which seemed ever to retreat. He clenched his teeth and spoke not, neither in agony nor in reproach, when the long search ended in vain. On the other hand a middle-aged man wept at having a cold poultice laid gently over a boil. Yet his daughter—pretty Dabal, whose teeth were pearly white because, like many of the modern young ladies, she refused to follow the fashion of her mother who thought that only teeth black from chewing betel could be beautiful—was patiently saving up cents with a view to going some day to the bazaar to have as many of her teeth as she could afford pulled out to be replaced with gold, a Chinese practice which fortunately few Dayaks so far have sought to copy.

The vivisection of a leg, the applying of a poultice and the drawing of teeth are trifling events compared to the cutting-off of a head, but they are brought in here deliberately, to throw doubt on a popular judgement. It is often said that 'primitive' people do not feel pain as much as Europeans. It has been said of the Land Dayaks.[1] Although it is incumbent upon a European observer to confirm a conclusion so pleasant to the conscience of his people if at all possible, in this case it is not possible to do so with any semblance of honesty. It is true that the Land Dayaks put up with much, but then there is much which they have to put up with. It is true, too, that some of them—but by no means all—file their front teeth to points believing that it makes them more beautiful. But the filing is done gradually, and would probably not be painful to anyone who had never been frightened by a dentist. Signs that the people do suffer in other ways may be noticed, if one takes particular care to be very, very observant. Babies cry, children sometimes scream or bellow, old men and women mourn, the whole religion turns on the prevention of sickness, and nearly everyone is afraid of the dark. Perhaps one may more often find death being accepted fatalistically, but then it must be remembered that such a fate is more familiar to the Dayaks.

Furthermore, it may only appear to be accepted fatalistically. The sufferer may in fact simply have turned to his last resource, that of self-pity, self-pity with a sacrificial flavour. The appreciation of martyrdom is useful to a peaceable society, and it is woven through the whole fabric of Land Dayak society as a thread giving it strength.

In particular there is an affliction known as *panun*. To explain completely its pathology would require a socio-medical treatise together with a dissertation on Dayak theology. Briefly, it is an affliction which comes upon one through failure to receive one's dues. The risk of it is kept before the people's minds by a simple form of etiquette. If a visitor calls at a home during a meal, he should be offered food. Failure to make the offer would endanger him. On the other hand, he places himself in danger if he fails to accept it, at least to the extent of touching it with his finger and then licking his finger. In fact, on ordinary occasions the matter is not treated very seriously. These occasions establish the ideal rather than oblige it. Although

---

[1] By a 'far-flung correspondent' in *The New Yorker*.

the offer is nearly always made, it is quite usual for the visitor to refuse it. The risk is his alone, and it is slight. The forces which rule the Dayak world do not expect perfection in daily life. At unimportant times rules may be broken fairly safely provided no one points them out. Of course, sometimes people are rude enough, or wily enough, to point them out. The girls make great play with a trick of this kind at festivals. They offer food, remind the victim of his obligation to take it, and then, when he reaches out his hand to touch it, contrive to leave such a quantity there that he is forced to over-eat himself.

Religious ceremonies are of greater moment, and it is here that the importance of giving and getting dues receives its strongest stress. Everyone present, to avoid the risk of *panun*, must receive a portion of the offerings. This, indeed, was a pleasant arrangement for me. In the United States, so I have heard, the anthropologist may have to pay fees to the Indians. The Dayaks, however, had to pay them to the anthropologist. At the end of every ceremony, I had to be given something—half a smoked fowl, some eggs, cooked *pulit* rice, or a bottle of wine, perhaps. Not only was I entitled to it. I had no choice but to accept it. And the people had no choice but to give it me. Otherwise I might have been bitten by a centipede, stung by a scorpion, snatched away by a demon, or fallen grievously sick. Then the fault would have been theirs, exposing them to public blame and a demand from me for compensation.

The idea that an injury is inflicted when an obligation is not fulfilled extends to any relationship in which somebody owes something to somebody else. The vast benefit to the community is clear. It simplifies the business of living by removing any need for shame at a meticulous insistence on one's rights. But of far greater importance is the fact that it gives all the power of supernatural backing to the ethic of contract upon which the people depend for the growing of their rice, the building of their homes and everything else which they accomplish by helping one another.

The idea, however, would not have much force unless the people were prone to look for the cause of suffering in the fault of others and to react to the fault of others with suffering. They are rather prone to do so. They are prone to a mood which psychologists might call a mild paranoia and which we shall call a sulk. Kichapi had a fit of sulking quite early in our Story when he was unable to do as he wished, and later on Bilantur sulked in his boat after he had been insulted. Whether this tendency comes from some deep spring in Land Dayak nature or whether it is simply a human tendency which the Dayaks tap, it is hard to say. On the whole I think it is the latter. One reason is that in the course of two years I did find the mood in question, like other Dayak moods, a trifle catchy. And it may have been catchy partly because of the second reason, which is the social value of such behaviour. Sulking, in Land Dayak eyes, is an affliction akin to sickness. It is therefore a useful resource. It takes the place of assault as a means of getting even with others, and it is much more satisfactory in its consequences. It does not break the relationship. It vivifies it. To the one sulking other people are very relevant. He can feel a new importance in their eyes as the person they have injured. If he ceased to feel this importance the sulk would lose its savour. In fact, the only practicable thing to do is to let it lose its savour. This is the course usually followed by the Dayaks. While showing him a modicum of concern, they leave the sulker very much to himelf, so as not to feed the mood. In due time he will revive, and then perhaps demand a fine to save his face.

Now the Land Dayaks do not very often sulk, and when they do they leave no one in any doubt about it, which is a virtue in itself. Nor do they fail to blame themselves almost as often as they do others. Nevertheless it is true that suffering does tend with them to have an accusative tinge. The accusation may be definite. But often the feeling is vaguer. It may provide a last consolation for the dying.

We cannot therefore answer the question as to whether the Dayaks suffer more or less than other people, or whether they are more or less brave. They bear their suffering rather differently and reconcile themselves to it by different means. What is certain is their keen wish to avoid it as far as they can. Their love of life is strong; their happiness precious to themselves. They have therefore a deep concern with the perils around, and they dare not forget them—which brings us back to the heads.

The heads hanging in the headhouse reflect into the people's minds a realistic picture of the world in which they live—a place of ever-present danger demanding vigilance, and perhaps struggle, for survival. It might be said that the picture is now unrealistic, and that the heads serve only to keep awake unnecessary fears. This may be so. But most villages prefer to keep some heads in their headhouses. They remain wary, and they may be wise to remain wary. Who can be sure that in their exposed land deep in South East Asia the danger has not merely receded soon to press upon them again.

In any case, a dangerous world is more exciting than a dull world—more pleasing, in a quivering sort of way, until the moment when decapitation appears imminent. The heads which hang in the head-house may frighten a little but also make aware, enliven, and unite the boys who go there to lie around, to talk, and ostensibly to sleep.

VII

BEYOND THE HEADHOUSE

WHEN darkness descended on the village of his Love, Kichapi left the headhouse. His power to command the darkness was more remarkable than his going abroad through it, for inmates of headhouses are prone to do so. Cautiously they venture forth in high excitement, padding softly on the longhouse floor, catlike in the night, seeking warm and companionable couches.

The companions they seek are women. It is love not loneliness which sends them forth, for the headhouse itself is a companionable place. Land Dayak boys and men, young with young and old with young, behave to one another with a freedom of friendly touch which, were they in our civilized society, might get them locked up in gaol. They pat each other, stroll with arms round each other, lie down embraced and often sleep together under the same covering. Yet, as far as I know, they always remain chaste in regard to one another. The Land Dayaks are highly homosocial but they are rarely, if ever, homosexual, and I believe that in the first fact may lie at least part of the reason for the second. From the beginning of their lives to the end they can indulge freely their affectionate feelings, especially the protective parental affection the older persons have for the younger, and these feelings therefore never reach the intensity which inspires sexual desire.

Sexual desire, to Dayak minds, is something which belongs exclusively to the love which men feel for women. In regard to love the Dayaks take an extreme view. Love is never platonic, using the word in its popular sense. It always involves sexual desire. Not that sexual desire is the be-all and end-all of Dayak love. It has a part in the history of each romance, but fond feelings may have given the romance birth, and when the desire weakens, the fond feelings may continue to bind enduringly.

The Dayak attitude to love has the advantage of giving people's minds the plainest direction and so keeping them unconfused. If sexual desire is assumed to enter into all love, it is assumed conversely to enter nowhere else. Thus other kinds of affection, of boys for boys, girls for girls, men for men, women for women, and the affection across the years which keeps the old young and the young secure, can be indulged freely and widely without thought of shame. Sexual desire has its clear and definite sphere. It is expected there, although it must be kept hidden. It is out of place anywhere else.

It is so much out of place that any display of their sexual characteristics by boys past the age of puberty in the presence of other boys and men is regarded as highly indecent. Probably nothing in European behaviour would shock Dayak men more than the sight of European men bathing unclothed. In Mentu Tapuh there was one poor crippled boy who always bathed alone upstream from the main bathing-place. I felt sorry for him, he being unable to take part in the playing and splashing which for the other boys formed the chief delight of the day. So I spoke to some of the people. It was by his own will, they said, that he stayed apart and rightly so. He had a withered arm. He could not therefore cover his genitals with one hand while he removed his garment with the other.

Some psychologists might argue that the taboo on displays of sexual characteristics in male company points to suppressed homosexual desires. I think they would be wrong. I think the explanation lies in the privacy of sex and the established canons of modesty. But here is not a suitable place to argue the question with them.

So much for ordinary affection. Let us now concern ourselves wholly with love. We said that the Dayak attitude is clear. When fondness for a girl is warmly expressed, or when it reaches a touching stage, its aim is sexual intimacy. Since the sexual act is regarded as in no way sinful in itself, although it may be wrong in particular instances, no one has any embarrassment in accepting this idea of love. At the same time, the ready acceptance of the idea leaves very little room for philandering with allegedly pure intent. The difference in the Dayak attitude from our own is that it is less openly hypocritical and more frank, but also more severe. This difference explains a feature of our Story which, without an understanding of it, could easily be misconstrued to the Dayaks' disadvantage. The way in which Kichapi behaved when he visited the ladies he loved is unblushingly described. Every English reader on reaching this account will, I feel sure, be inclined to snap the book shut. The Dayaks would not be at all shocked by the description. Yet this does not mean that the

Dayaks believe in unrestricted love. They are not less moral in this respect. Kichapi's loving is not necessarily condoned. Certainly similar loving of young men in their own village is not publicly condoned. But once the listeners have heard that Kichapi did intend to love, then they would expect him to behave as he did. The difference in attitude is not really very great. It is merely a question of where the line is drawn. In regard to fondling love, we accept, or pretend to accept, a principle of 'thus far and no further'. The Dayaks accept, or pretend to accept, a principle of 'no advance at all'. The parallel to Dayak morality in our culture is that of the Divorce Court judge.

Because love is unambiguous, any expressions of it in public, other than verbal play, are considered bad form. Dayaks would be surprised by behaviour in an English park. They must be much more circumspect in their petting. On days when paddy fields are planted the young men and women, when the work is done, seize each member of their party to blacken him or her with the charcoal left by the burning of the cut bush on the field. There are chances then in the contrived accidents of struggle for the quick fondling of breasts. There are chances, too, for like manoeuvres during bathing. But otherwise day-time opportunities are few.

Even married couples should be circumspect. One night at a festival a man I knew well sitting beside me whispered, nodding his head in the direction of a middle-aged villager, 'He's a funny man.'

'Why?'

'He's always with his wife,' he said. 'He goes always to the paddy fields where she is working, never to different paddy fields. And look at him now. Sitting right beside her!'

Actually there was more in this particular case than met the eye. The couple were not behaving indecently. They were not even holding hands. The charge implied against the husband was that he was showing himself jealous, but his behaviour on this occasion hardly merited the charge. I think the friend who made it was in fact seeking through his censure of the man the comfort of superior virtue for his own wounded feelings. Earlier in the evening his own wife had come up to him to announce, 'I am going to play a little. Don't be angry with me', and then, before he could answer, whisked herself away into a group of young women who were dancing and teasing young men. I watched her. She did play. She overplayed. Later he was angry. Then she was angry. Neither of them were angry in public, but the whole village got to hear of it. Smouldering still the next night, she barred the door of his own house against him, shutting him out as ignominiously as the man who became the moon was shut out by the woman who became the nightjar. All this was very hard on my friend. The premonition of it no doubt inspired his remark.

He himself might, in the eyes of heaven, have been excused a little jealousy. His wife was the second loveliest, although not the second nicest, girl in the village. The loveliest was her cousin. They were two beauties who, with their parents, had migrated to this Sarawak village to escape from the Dutch, that is to say, from the Dutch system of administration. He might, then, have been excused a little jealousy, but only in the eyes of heaven. Jealousy cannot be excused lightly by the members of a small community. Love is a form of selfishness *à deux*. It is best kept out of public life.

But married people are, after all, declared lovers. With unmarried persons there is a far more important reason for insisting on circumspection in their loving. This lies in the certain meaning which the Dayaks give to love, namely that it implies sexual desire. The Dayaks do not underrate the pleasures which come from this desire: far from it. They are not puritanical in the popular sense of the word. But they hold that the right place for these pleasures is in the permanent declared unions which will provide care for the offspring. They well know that this is not the only place. But by not openly recognizing the other places, the society can bring pressure to bear on persons whose behaviour becomes scandalous or is childish in its results. Any sound society does as much. But the Dayaks in fact allow a greater freedom to young love than do some societies. There is thus a greater need for it to be kept out of sight.

Keeping it out of sight does not mean denying it. In the interests of social order, unmarried love must be held to be wrong. At the same time no one is in any doubt about human nature and no one has any wish to restrain it harshly in the young. The apparent contradiction in this situation is avoided by means of a great connivance. What is publicly condemned is privately tolerated. It may be more than tolerated. It may be positively aided, but always with enough duplicity for it to be overlooked. Overlooking is indeed the essence of the connivance. The public, however, cannot avert its eye from obvious breaches of its code. The young must co-operate by keeping their illicit affairs away from its eye. This is why there is such a very great need for them to be circumspect.

The need comes with puberty. Earlier than this the children, called singly and collectively *baduput*, go about clothed or unclothed at will. Little attention is paid to their distinguishing sexual characteristics save that those of the boys are very occasionally made the subject of teasing. The children are soon aware of the nature of sexual activity but regard it, for the most part, as something into which they will grow. They have a modicum of modesty, or are taught it. They would be corrected if they played sexually in public, but they never seem to do so. No one worries about what they might do in private. There is no need for anyone to worry because the children are so rarely in private. Boys go about in groups and girls go about in groups, and groups of each kind rarely mix except now and then in games which generally end in quarrels brought about by the boys becoming rough with the girls.

Often the roughness is deliberate. There is no constant antipathy between boys and girls, however. Generally they are friendly. Sometimes they have a relationship which is truly gentle. Laiyau was chivalrous to Kudor. Were they at my house together at night, he would leave when she wished to leave in order to accompany her home across the dark village. One day I asked him if he intended to marry her. He replied, almost regretfully I thought, that he could never do so as she was his first cousin. Had she been his second cousin marriage could have been possible. Had she been any less closely related it could have been fully approved, although of course it would have required postponing.

Laiyau and Kudor were almost past the stage of being children. They had almost reached the stage of puberty. With this stage a boy becomes entitled to impose a fine upon anyone who even speaks jokingly of his genitals. For his part he is most careful to keep them covered from sight, being as particular in male company as in female. Girls at the same stage show an equal concern for personal privacy. From an earlier age than the boys they have usually avoided being unclothed in the view of others but now it becomes invariable for them to wear sarongs, however short and patched their sarongs may be. For with puberty the boys and girls are no longer regarded as *baduput*, or children. They have become *bujang*, or young men and young ladies—very young ones, still far short of marriage, but entering the world of love.

A certain mystery, befitting it, surrounds this world of love, especially in its sunrise, which I cannot, even if I wished, pretend to dispel. Of course I tried to find out all I could about it, but in such a deeply personal matter the eyes are of little help and talk is notoriously misleading. Anthropologists of high repute often do speak with certainty of the intimate lives of their chosen people, but I feel that in this respect they must either be departing from their usual high standards of first-hand observation or else they must be men or women who deserve to rate as remarkable in any society. What follows therefore is not statistical but speculative. It is speculative because Dayak love defeated scientific method.

Some say that young boys get their first initiation into love from young ladies a few years their senior, who thereby get their own first initiation. For the boys it is a tutoring, for the girls a dalliance, a prelude to the more serious affairs into which they will graduate when they have gained confidence. I do not know whether this is true. Certainly a boy does first attract the attention of girls older than himself. Tuntong was a case in point.

Tuntong, the boy from Suhu, was about eleven years old when he came to live in my house. One could only guess at his age. A Dayak is in truth as old as he looks or feels, for there is no counting of birthdays. Apart from children born during my stay, or shortly before, there was only Grandfather Ichau in the whole village of whose age I could be certain. He was exceptional also in being certain of it himself. He was proud to have it known that he was seventy-seven. A skilful boatman, capable of paddling down to Serian and back again as quickly as anyone; the leading politician, priest, judge, capitalist and primary producer; the benign grandfather of some of the lustiest and loveliest children and yet the not-so-long wedded husband of his fourth wife, having survived the other three in succession—he had cause for his pride if such were his age. But in fact the very basis of his claim proved him wrong. He was born, he said, 'on the morning after the day on which the world shook'. The event which shook the world to herald Grandfather Ichau's birth was the explosion of Krakatoa, and it took place in 1883. He was, therefore, in 1950, only sixty-seven. He spoke always in good faith, so I would content myself by expressing a wish that he would live to be a hundred and ten.

There was no Krakatoa to date Tuntong. When he came to Mentu Tapuh, I assessed him on his looks at eleven. His looks changed. He grew like a beanstalk. He was at an age for growing, but that could hardly account for his phenomenal growth. It may have been his diet, which had much more meat in it than Dayaks ordinarily have. It may have been that he was kept free from malaria during this period. At any rate, Tuntong who was eleven in the middle of 1949 was by the middle of 1950 an exceptionally tall thirteen.

When I remarked one day to Nyandoh on the way in which Tuntong had grown he said, 'Yes. It fills me with surprise. A while ago he was nobody. Now in the paddy fields all the girls talk of him.' The girls who talked of Tuntong were not all of a like age to him. Some were fifteen or sixteen or even seventeen years old. Their talk on the face of it seemed innocent enough. But it sprang from a ground of tender interest and amidst the lush general gossip about his doings were small teasing allegations of love.

Allegations of this kind are not always repudiated. Boys or girls may boldly assert an attachment, to a person who may or may not boldly reciprocate. As real love is notoriously secret, their boldness makes it clear that they are playing a game. Often they are doing so. If in any case they are not, their boldness makes it seem so, which protects them from scandal while at the same time enlarging their opportunities. I am not suggesting that this device is purely Dayak, but merely that the Dayaks make good use of it. A few boys nowadays get the name of a girl tattooed on their arm. This is a testimony, however, to their egotism rather than to their love. It is a literary conceit developed, whether their teachers know it or not, among boys at the Mission school. Tuntong could neither read nor write and did not pretend to prove by a single word that he could. Nevertheless he startled me by philandering with Lupan, a full-breasted girl who looked at least his very big sister if not quite old enough to be his mother.

Such semi-public play is permissible because it is assumed to be only play. If in fact it is sometimes more, and I have no proof that it is, little harm is done and probably some good. It would be a gentle way of learning love, useful practice in an art which must be silent, and a protection for the younger girls whose readiness for lessons develops more slowly than that of boys of the same age, who are more ardent and less delicate.

A girl like Lupan spends but a short time in the kindergarten of love. Very soon she blossoms into a complete young lady, looked upon rosily by everyone except perhaps her rivals. If the years go by and she does not marry, she will, as maidens do anywhere, lose a little of her fresh-blown charm, but for a year or two, or even more, she will

G

be a hard-working village princess. Gumiloh was such a princess.
So too was Kumang Malidi, her viceroy in Kichapi's heart.

This indeed is the most glorious period in life for these maidens—
let no one cast a slur upon them. Their names are constantly upon
people's lips. Their household's paddy field is named after them, and
the fields where they work are favoured, gay places. To festivals they
bring a brightness more essential than that of the lamps, and even
ordinary nights they illumine, each for her own little circle of admirers,
or with a companion to share her regency when they hold court
in their own homes, or when they mix into groups with the young men
on the longhouse verandah. Then they engage in conversation or in
singing, both of which involve much prior thought, cleverness and skill.

Sometimes the cleverness extends to the means. Early one morning
when the Catholic missionary was visiting the village our own much
less clever conversation brought us into an argument as to whether
or not the Land Dayaks had any night-life. We decided to go up on to
the longhouse for an on-the-spot investigation. The verandah was in
darkness. But it was not deserted. At the nearer end we stumbled into
a group of young men behaving mysteriously. They were huddled
close together. They would sing awhile; then pause as quiet as frozen
mice; then sing again. At first they seemed to be singing to themselves.
Then we discovered that they were singing to a fine membrane of
deerskin. From this membrane stretched a very thin fibre of vine.
We followed it down the whole length of the verandah, and there
at the far end we found what we expected, for we had already been
let into the secret,—a group of girls singing to another membrane.
The young men and young women had a name for their device.
They called it a *telifon*.

The songs they were singing were like the following:

> *Nabang gawang tumbuh tabeng ayih*
> *Kulit nya kana titih tupai dua—*
> *Mayoh bintang tumbuh dalam langih,*
> *Ajah pidujuh ayih mata,*
> *Ajah piluruh tangkai nyawa.*

> Even a tree chopped down beside a stream
> Has had its bark all scratched by squirrels paired—
> A million stars are twinkling in the sky,
> But yet the tears are dropping from my eyes,
> And only sadness wells up within my heart.

Verses, or complete small songs, are bandied back and forth between the girls and boys, making up a language of love.

It is a language which may be openly spoken because it is not spoken to solitary ears. All the pastimes so far mentioned—the evening visiting, the clever conversations and the singing contests—are party pleasures. There are no courting couples. Love in the public purview must be love in the plural. We have explained why this is so. It is so in order that a happy compromise may be kept between what is and what ought to be. But there are other pastimes which are strictly private, which must be kept private at the partakers' peril. Which brings us back to the excursions from the headhouse.

Everyone knows that in the silence of the night girls may welcome single lovers. Everyone knows it although no one admits it of the girls they know. The encounters must be carefully pre-arranged. Often a young man will get another girl or an older woman to sound out a girl who he thinks, sometimes because of indications given by the girl herself, may favour him, perhaps asking his agent to convey a gift. The gift may be anything from a coloured sarong, for the luckiest girl, to a cake of soap. Often there is no gift at all. But few men would be as bold as Kichapi in approaching his chosen ones without any pre-arrangement. The doings of an ordinary lover would be much the same, however, save that he would enter by the door instead of dropping down from the roof.

He must enter carefully, for he is on a dangerous expedition. He runs the risk of being caught by his beloved's mother, and after the catching will come a fine, and with the fine will come the great shame of exposure. Yet the risk is not as great as it might be. The room is not set out as a trap. On the contrary, it is usually arranged to facilitate his deed. We spoke before of how the society connives to give liberty to the love it must forbid. Here the connivance is at its most transparent. Girls are not supposed to receive lovers. Yet when they reach the age at which it becomes most likely that they shall, they are given beds separate from the common bed of the rest of the family. There are excuses for this, of course, some of which are reasonable. The parents themselves may feel easier away from their older children. The older boys sleep separately in the headhouse. But it is most noticeable that the beds of the girls are generally far removed from those of their parents and are often set strategically close to the door from the longhouse verandah. It is most noticeable, but it is very bad taste to point it out.

Why, then, need young men fear intervention from parents? There are several reasons why they may intervene. Perhaps the affairs have been whispered about, and the parents wish to scotch the scandals before they grow. To avoid this risk a young man is wise to keep his intentions secret even from his friends. Mere silence may not be enough. If he is clever, he may seek actively to divert suspicion. He may, for instance, spend the evening in conversation with a girl different from the one upon whom he has designs. To courage and a catlike skill, therefore, we must add a certain cunning as a requirement for successful adventure.

Another reason for intervention is one which is often thought to be stronger than it is, for the more a young man believes in it the more he can preen himself. It is often real, however. It is that the parents may see in the visitor a desirable match for their daughter. Sometimes the daughter has the duplicity to aid in the catching. On the second time he visited a girl, said one young man, he was soothed quite to sleep. He awoke in the early dawn to see his beloved bending over the fire cooking the family breakfast. He escaped never to return. We may, therefore, add a further requirement for success—a wariness about the wiles of love.

The young man was on only his second visit. To him this was the most shocking feature of the affair, because on that score he could expect to be fairly safe. But the more frequent visits to the same girl become, the more the danger rises. For the reason why parents may intervene, by their own will or through the contrivance of their daughter, concerns pregnancy. The intention may be either to prevent it or to fix responsibility for it. In regard to pregnancy the Dayaks have definite views, strange though they may be to some of us. They believe that a single act of intercourse cannot make a woman pregnant. Nor can two acts, nor three. To produce a child a man and woman must consort over a period of months. Their theory is a plausible one. It is soundly based upon statistical probability, and there are few cases to conflict with it because the need for secrecy in casual affairs generally results in a relatively low statistic in regard to any one girl until a considerable period has elapsed.

The defect of the theory is that it may impose an unfairness upon a girl. This may force her to act unfairly in self-defence. The result is a suspicion between the sexes, a suspicion, however, which at least has the virtue of encouraging caution. Because the theory leaves no easy alternative, a girl who sleeps with a man on just a few occasions and then becomes pregnant may be held to have had a previous lover. If she then holds her present lover responsible, it may be alleged that she does so in order to make him a scapegoat or because he is a better catch. There may sometimes be truth in the allegation. It may be that the girl has had a previous lover who disclaimed responsibility, or who was married. The latter eventuality is uncommon because although a few Dayaks, like many Europeans—like most Americans, if we take Dr Kinsey's word—are unfaithful, they generally prefer to be unfaithful with unfaithful women, leaving the young to the young. Or it may be that the girl discovers her forthcoming motherhood after she has forsaken her old association and begun her new. There may, then, sometimes be truth in the allegation. But in most cases there is probably not. The girl is simply the victim of an unrecognized chance of biology.

Even so, her fate is rarely sad. In the first place, love is by no means always inclined to go by theory and affection may over-ride concern about the earliness of a pregnancy. Secondly, the girl can accuse, and her accusations are feared. They are feared for several reasons. A man faces shame if he claims that his association was shortlived, because it should not have been lived at all. His best hope lies in complete denial. This is difficult. The scales are weighted heavily against him. Although there is honesty and restraint and much maidenliness in the Dayak female character, there is little of the innocence which we often misconstrue as a virtue. Should a girl be fickle, she will probably have contrived to let her association with her present lover be known, or rumoured, before she tells him she is pregnant. Indeed even good girls are generally wise enough to keep quiet until the time for fair doubt of responsibility has passed, which is a main reason why cases of disputed parenthood seldom arise. But a good girl may be less guarded, or a fickle man may give her no opportunity for constancy. Then her name for virtue will help her in her trouble. Thus it happens that bad girls tend to protect themselves and good girls tend to be protected by their reputations.

There are other weights, too, always on the girl's side of the scales. The child in her womb is the heaviest. If only the accused is named, upon whom else can the blame be laid? If the accused does try to blame someone else, then he faces two denials against his one. There is also the weight of male sentiment. Although men may make implications against women in general, in any particular case not involving themselves they tend to give their sympathy to the woman.

Perhaps the women themselves incline the other way. I do not know. And it does not matter, because all cases which come up for public settlement are settled by the men.

There are further dangers in denial, especially for a man who does not feel very sure of his ground. Can he be certain that the fates will not decree against him? There is one lesson before the minds of all Mentu Tapuh men. About twenty years ago a young woman accused a man of being the father of her unborn child. He denied the charge dramatically. Into the presence of a group of villagers he brought a frog, and reminding them of the belief that the deliberate cutting of an animal, dead or alive, or the breaking of its limbs, by an expectant father may result in his child's being born deformed, he severed one of the frog's legs. In due course the child was born. The top joints of two of its fingers were missing. A perfectly formed child may not have proved his innocence. A deformed child convincingly proved him guilty. He left the village. The incident happened twenty years ago, but the three-fingered child, now a three-fingered married woman, remains in the community, a warning to all who would garnish guilt with arrogance.

Cases of disputed parenthood are in fact few, and none of them are of much lasting importance. There are not very many illegitimate children in Mentu Tapuh, or rather, to put it the way the Dayaks think of it, there are not very many illegitimate parents. There are no children at all without recognized fathers. It may be that some few men have felt in their hearts that fatherhood has been wrongly thrust upon them, but they keep the feeling in their hearts, or banish it altogether, once the public judgement has gone against them. The reason is simple. It is that although a man may be reluctant to take a particular woman as his wife, all Dayak men keenly want children.

For this same reason a man who does feel responsible for a woman's coming motherhood rarely if ever attempts to deny it. The situation is happier for him, of course, for only with a woman pleasant to him would he have lain often enough to feel sure of his responsibility. Indeed, Land Dayak pre-marital loving can be properly understood only in terms of the desire for children. True, it cannot all be explained away as trial marriage. Some young men sample a little too widely for that. But their early adventures are usually short and spasmodic and with young girls, and therefore of little account. Whether because of youngness or because the affairs are short and spasmodic, young girls do not often become pregnant.

There may be many young girls who run no risk whatever of pregnancy. It would distress me to leave an impression that the Land Dayaks are promiscuous. This would be most unfair to them. For all I know, some girls may be virginal until they go to their marriage beds. A lot may be so until they meet their husbands-to-be. For the rest, their early trials of love soon pass, through deepening attachments, into trials at family as well. They wish to marry when they know their marriages will be fruitful.

For a while I thought that this could not generally be the case, because of the number of childless couples. It was clear enough that older men, persistently childless, might marry simply to gain a help-mate and companion. But there were some quite young married men who were also without children. Machan was one of them. In his even younger days he, so it was said, had had a particularly roving eye, and yet here he was, while still young enough to have let it rove a little longer, if not exactly settled down at least living constantly with a wife in a house unblessed with son or daughter. Later I learnt that Machan and his wife were not in fact untypical. They were merely unlucky. Their child was still-born. Other childless couples have suffered similarly. Their children had not been born alive, or had died, as so many children do. These cases add essentially to the picture of Land Dayak love. They show that although men and women wish to have their marriages fruitful, marriage has for them all a meaning more than its fruit. It is a contract between two persons founded upon an attachment which often binds them closer over the years. Of course the contract is more easily and lightly broken if the couple remain childless. Machan was not quite settled. Children strengthen a marriage and much more often than not en-sure that it will last a lifetime.

The contract itself is simply sealed. It is not intended to be binding to the point of pain. It is not a religious occasion, like birth or death. In the house of the bridegroom's family, or of the bride's family, depending upon where the two have taken up their residence, which they will have done prior to the occasion, there will be a gathering of friends, attended also by a number of the leading old men of the village. There will be feasting and drinking on a modest scale. When edges have gone from appetites and the wine has lubricated tongues, the old men will orate a little, or debate a little, about the good life and how it should be led to promote wedded bliss and preserve the peace of the community. The father of the bridegroom accedes to the marriage, in which he generally has had no say, after perhaps making a few derogatory remarks about his son. The father of the bride, who also usually has had no influence on the making of the marriage, accedes without the unkindness. The mothers say nothing. The husband and wife each testify briefly to the strength of their love and to the goodness of their intentions. Thus the matter is settled, and the feasting may continue without further distraction into the night. Until after the fourth night following the wedding, including that on which it takes place, the couple must stay at home. Their honeymoon is thus an enforced experiment in domesticity. Neither of them is likely to be very young. The wife will seldom be under eighteen. She may often be nineteen or twenty or more. Her husband is likely to be slightly older.

The marriage completed, we may cast a quick backward glance over what may have been its prelude. For the man there may have been adventures from the headhouse, for the woman adventures in her own home. The element of adventure is highly important. For the young adventure is the salt of life. The adventure they have through love is more than physically satisfying. It is soul-satisfying as well. Ardent spirits cannot rest content under constraint. They need to defy, now and then, ordinary rules, for the sake of morale. In the Dayak world of today the pursuit of love and, for the very bold, challenges to religious restrictions provide them with the main and almost sufficient means of defiance. The supernatural can cope with the challenges, and the society can cope with the love. By doing so, it possibly saves itself much trouble, and it certainly saves the young much trial. If they come to the fulfilment of passion early, who can regret it, when their lives are often sadly short? No one is harmed, or if a few are harmed the casualties are probably less in number and less severe than in most forms of loving. All this, however, is now threatened by the missionaries. They are very good men, intending and achieving much good, but I cannot refrain from wishing that they could be a little less urgently interested in sex.

The Dayaks do not regard the sexual adventures of the young as immoral, in the sense in which the missionaries might regard them as immoral. They do not regard them as wrong and yet they cannot regard them as right. The essence of the matter is that they should not be regarded at all. A veil should be drawn over them to protect them from the face of the society.

The veil is withdrawn in the Story, to give all a chance to hear and know the nature of reality. The Story may shock a Western reader. I hope it will not, but it may, because our hypocrisy is of a slightly different order, suited perhaps to our different society. Yet, in Dayak terms, how very moral a tale the Story really is! Kichapi shared his first adventures with two lovely sisters. He was strong and virile and exceptional in taking two. But at the end of the Story he married both. He never changed his loves, and he lived with them happily ever after.

VIII

CONCLUSION

WE have been brought right back to the Story and there is but one more feature of it which needs explaining before we go on to enjoy it. This feature, which provides a contrast with many modern European tales of fact and fiction, is the small concern shown for 'character', either psychologically or morally. Yet the Story does teach both a psychological and a moral lesson, slight though both lessons are.

The Dayaks are not much inclined to speculate about why people behave as they do. In the Story, actions, often contradictory actions such as those of the Dragon-chief in first welcoming Kichapi and then immediately hurling at him a spear as broad-bladed as a palm frond, are accepted at their face value. This is very different from the attitude of most of us, and certainly very different from the attitude of many of our novelists. There is a simple reason for the difference. In our crowded and wide society we can generally choose our company, and we can escape from it, if necessary by going to Borneo. Insight can help us to choose well and to know when to escape. In the tiny society of the Dayak village, on the other hand, all the people must perforce live together, and naturally they wish to do so as happily as possible. Their happiness could not be increased by their bothering about the inner thoughts of their companions. It is quite enough to have to reckon with what they do and say. The good commonsense the Dayaks show in this regard is reflected in the Story.

What, then, is the psychological lesson of the Story? It is clear enough. The less the people calculate character the more watchful they need to be in regard to actions. They must be on guard against the unexpected. In any case, in the dangerous Dayak world watchfulness is much safer than calculation, which may be misleading. The Story stresses the need for watchfulness. It teaches the value of mistrust.

The difference in Dayak attitude from our own is, of course, only one of degree. Literature sharpens tendencies. Few of us in ordinary life psychologize as persistently as do our novelists, and few Dayaks

are as persistently mistrustful as Kichapi. I should hate, indeed, to leave
the impression that any of them are mistrustful generally. They trust
their friends, and if they come to trust them slowly and continue
always to respect the privacy of their minds, they are not themselves
the poorer friends thereby. We have overlooked, too, the most important reason why Dayaks do not show very much concern about
each other's natures. It is that they do not often need to do so, because
nearly all of them are good-natured.

What, now, of the moral aspect of the Story? There are no clear
heroes and villains. It is hard to distinguish between the characters
according to any criterion of virtue. On the bad side we could perhaps
put the enemies of Kichapi, and on the good side himself and his
friends. But the case for doing so is slender. The first enemy,
Minyawai, was a great killer, but so, too, was Kichapi. The second
enemy, Bilantur, was nothing worse than a fool, a badly-treated
fool who was provoked into doing all that he did. It is true, however,
that both these two were attackers and so might be classed as bad
on that account, but only on that account. Still less clear is the position
of Singiyang Naga, the Dragon-chief. He was a cunning creature, a
would-be murderer of Kichapi, yet his generous host and powerful
ally.

Turning now to the supposedly good side, what right has Kichapi to
be there? He is hardly a shining exemplar to the Dayak young. He
seduced maidens. We have made out a case for him on that account,
proving him virtuous in the end, but still his actions in the short run
were not of the kind the public could approve. And look what else
he did! He raged, he sulked, he tricked his benefactors and he stole
from them. But I do not wish to make him out as too bad. There was a
lot of good in him. He supported his friends, he never forgot his
parents, he provided solace for his brothers and he settled down with
his wives.

There was obvious good in him. But there was also a lot in him of
which the goodness was not so obvious. He accepted no restraints.
He defied the laws of men and gods. By doing so, he excites wondrous
admiration, because his boldness and power are beyond the dreams of
ordinary men.

To our minds there might seem to be little good in such defiance
and in boldness so directed. Is the tale, then, immoral? For Dayak
minds it is not. Let us consider again the bad side of Kichapi. His
misdeeds confer the same kind of benefit upon the hearers of the tale

as the crime stories which fill our newspapers do upon their readers. They help to keep people good by providing them with a vicarious delight in wrong. Kichapi does for others what they might not dare to do for themselves.

But why are these others not encouraged to dare by such an example? In the crime stories the criminal comes, or is felt likely to come, to a nasty end. Kichapi escapes such an end. He escapes, however, only because of his superhuman power. He is strong in body, of outstanding courage, and fortified by magic. From the impression of his power which it builds up comes the greatest benefit of the Story. The things at which so strong a man tilts cannot be windmills. And so the standards of the society are enhanced, or at least protected, by the extraordinary power shown to be necessary to disrespect them.

The Story fits Dayak morality better than it does our own, which is differently conceived. Not that the difference is really very great. Both moralities have their source in human nature, which alone is sufficient for the simpler virtues, and both have a supernatural sanction. But whereas under our Christian ideology the supernatural holds the human heart responsible to it, under the Dayak ideology it exercises its power more directly. The Dayaks therefore rely less on personal condemnation and have a greater regard for the ordained law. This attitude the Story supports.

All this we may argue plausibly, but in doing so we are making too much of a minor matter. We said the lessons of the tale are slight, and slight they are indeed. The Story has a far greater worth than the teaching of lessons, which are but dull steps to happiness. Its aim is direct—to while away the night, to lighten the labour in the fields, to please and to excite. In other words, the Story is meant, first and last, to entertain.

THE STORY OF KICHAPI

(As told by Raseh, in Kampong Mentu Tapuh, on the night of 22 November 1950 and on the eight following nights)

THE STORY OF KICHAPI

His Birth and First Encounters with the Giants

THIS is the story of a boy. His father's name was Sunang. His mother's name was Rigih. His grandfather's name was Saer. His grandmother's name was Samang. The name which he was first given was Silanting Kuning.[1] He was born in a village between Sangau and Pontianak.

His mother was pregnant with him for seven years and seven months. Her labour lasted seven days.[2] When he was born, he had with him a knife, a spear, a blowpipe, a shield, and a brass cooking pot.

While his mother was still lying by the fire after his birth, he walked off with his elder brother to the house where the heads of enemies are kept in order to join the older boys and unmarried men, who by Dayak custom sleep there at nights.

The next day a Gura bird, with all its feathers of gold, perched on a flowering tree near the headhouse.[3] Silanting Kuning shot at it with his blowpipe. It was wounded, and fell down, but when he went to pick it up, it flew away.

Silanting Kuning went after the bird. He kept on chasing it the whole day, but he could not catch it. So in the late afternoon he returned to the headhouse to collect his belongings—his knife, his spear, his blowpipe, his shield, and his brass cooking pot—and then he set off again. At dusk he found the bird dead, and he ate it raw.

Night came on, and in the darkness he lost his way. Crying, he lay down at the foot of a big tree and fell asleep. In his dream, a giant came towards him—an *Antu Muta*, the kind of giant who has seven heads. The giant sang as he came along:

[1] A land Dayak child may have his or her name changed for various reasons, the most usual of which is sickness. It is considered that better fortune may attend the new name. Changes after adulthood are less frequent, for personal names then fall out of general use in favour of teknonyms.

[2] Seven is regarded as a significant number by the Land Dayaks, although whether this significance is for good or ill may depend on context and is not always clear. It is regarded as a particularly good omen to have seven children provided they are all of the one sex. After seven, five is the most significant number.

[3] The colours of this bird are normally red, white and black.

'*O am bau jiluma bau anak munsea!*
Baih telan kami tukuh biradih!'

'Ah, the smell of a boy, the smell of a child!
So nice for us seven brethren to swallow!'

Silanting Kuning answered the giant with the song:

'*O am Antu Muta pirapa raya!*
Telan aku toh telan,
Aku tuh chunchu Saer biduan Samang,
Anak Rigih biduan Sunang.
Chuba ku ngasa ipuh ima sibarang bisa,
Ipuh sudi bilayang mandi;
Sumpit ku kena lalu mati,
Ndah kena mati buruk.'

'Oh, Seven-headed Giant from the vast swamp!
Swallow me, swallow me if you must,
But[1] I'm the grandchild of Saer and Samang,
The child of Rigih and Sunang.
Let me show the power of my blowpipe arrow,
An arrow which may fly straight or wide;
For if I make a hit, the victim falls dead,
If missed, it dies of wounds.'

Thereupon the giant said that, such being the case, he had no wish to swallow him. Instead he would give him the most powerful of all medicine to make him brave. The giant gave him the medicine, and went away.

Dawn came. Silanting Kuning awoke. He wept. Then he started to walk. As he went along, he sang to himself:

---

[1] The passage 'if you must, but' is an addition to the translation not appearing in the original. Land Dayaks often do not express a contra-positive which is implied by a context. Failure to appreciate this linguistic form can result in personal misunderstandings, for a stranger may regard a statement as an affirmation when in fact it is a premiss to a disagreement.

PLATE V

Above: Grandfather Ichau tells stories to his grandchildren pausing for a smoke of home-grown tobacco in his bamboo pipe. The pictures on the longhouse wall have come from newspapers and magazines in the writer's house.

Below: Miyah, a young married woman, and a young relative, return from their household's garden with sugar-cane in their canoe and a basket of dry bamboo for firewood.

'*Bijalai anchah anchai bijalai,*
Ku ajah nait munguh turun munguh,
Munguh ada biribu lapan;
Namu sungai duah bitanchang,
Namu danau duah bitingang.'

'Walking on, for ever walking,
Uphill I go, and downhill,
On hills of a thousand different kinds;
Each stream at its mouth flows into a second,
Each lake at its end joins another.'

Night came and, as before, Silanting Kuning lay down to sleep at the foot of a big tree.

In his dream a different kind of giant came along—an *Antu Bilitu.* This giant, too, sang as he came towards him:

'Ah, the smell of a boy, the smell of a child!
So nice for us seven brethren to swallow!'

Silanting Kuning sang in answer:

'*O am Antu Bilitu,*
Bigiling jaju bitungkat kayu!
Antu kambah ngilabah!
Antu buau ngilabau!
Telan aku toh telan'

'Oh, Bilitu Giant,
With your head turned back to front, and your staff of wood!
Giant of great deceit!
Giant of many lies!
Swallow me, swallow me if you must'

and then he went on as he had done to the other giant.

The giant replied as the first one had done, and gave Silanting Kuning medicine to make him brave, saying that he would regard him as his grandson.

Once more dawn came, and on and on walked Silanting Kuning

PLATE VI
Above: Tuntong
Below: Dabal

H

crying and singing his song. He came to a mountain—a mountain as high as the one here at Mentu Tapuh[1]—and went right up to the top.

There he met another giant of the seven-headed kind, and the giant's wife. They were gathering the big species of rattan vine. Silanting Kuning said to them:

"What are the two of you doing?"

"We are pulling down this big rattan vine."

"How long have you been at it?"

"Four days."

"Well, then," said Silanting Kuning, "that shows that you giants cannot be nearly as strong as men."

The male giant thereupon said to him, "All right, try to pull it down yourself, and if you don't succeed, I will swallow you."

Silanting Kuning tried. With one pull he brought the whole vine tumbling in coils to the ground. The giants were amazed, and the husband said to him, while his wife agreed:

"Oh, my! You are very strong indeed. You must become our grandson, and come home with us."

So Silanting Kuning went with them to their house, which was built inside a big cave. When he got inside the house, the giant and his wife said to each other that they must make sure he could not escape. They agreed that the best of all ways to make sure was to eat him. So the husband swallowed him. But Silanting Kuning immediately slipped right through his body. Then the giantess tried, and he slipped right through her. The giant tried again, with the same result. Seven times the husband tried and seven times the wife tried, but neither could keep him inside his or her stomach.

Having failed, they began to like him. They liked him so much that they decided that he need never walk. They would show their fondness for him by carrying him everywhere on their backs. The giant and giantess took him on a hunting trip. His new grandfather carried him all the way on his back. They speared deer, wild pig, barking-deer, mouse-deer, and other animals. When it came time for their return, his new grandmother carried him on her back.

When they arrived home, they did not cook the animals but ate them raw.

After this excursion the giants said that in future Silanting Kuning must stay at home. They made him promise that when they were

[1] A jungle-clad limestone peak about 2,000 ft above the level of the village.

away he would never climb the areca palm which was growing in front of the outer verandah of their house.[1]

Silanting Kuning stayed one year with these giants, sleeping in the same bed with them and eating the same food. He never climbed the areca palm. But each day, while his grandfather and his grandmother were out working in the countryside, he wondered why they had forbidden him to climb it. One day he decided to find out by climbing it.

All day he climbed, for as he climbed the palm grew higher, and the higher he climbed the higher it grew. At last he reached the top. Then he found that the palm had really curved over, and that the top rested on the roof of a longhouse, in a village far away from where he had begun his climb. As he looked down on to this longhouse, he saw on the verandah a most beautiful girl, drying her paddy in the sun. The name of this girl was Gumiloh.

Silanting Kuning meets Gumiloh

When Silanting Kuning saw Gumiloh, he said to himself: "What a very pretty girl!"

He plucked an areca-nut, stuck his small knife into it and threw it so it landed in the middle of the paddy which she was drying.

Gumiloh started back in anger, exclaiming: "Oh, drat! Here am I mourning for my dead father, who was killed by his enemy Minyawai from another village. And now comes some stranger to disturb me." But she could not spy where Silanting Kuning was.

Silanting Kuning climbed down the areca palm and went back to the giants' house. When he got there he wept, because he was in love with Gumiloh, who was so pretty. His grandparents had not yet returned from their work in the countryside. He was angry with them for having forbidden him to climb the palm. So he locked the doors of the house to shut them out.

The giants came back home. They found themselves locked out of their house. They called and called, but got no answer, and they could see no sign of Silanting Kuning. They agreed with each other as to what must have happened. They said that he must already have climbed the areca palm and was angry with them for having stopped him doing so before.

[1] The house was apparently built in Land Dayak style, just as if it were one household section of a longhouse.

When Silanting Kuning heard them talking to each other in this way he opened the door for them. But he would not speak to them, and went straight off to bed. He stayed in bed a whole day. He would not touch a bite of food. At last his grandparents picked him up, took him to the bathing-place and gave him a bath. They then said, "Well, if you are going to behave like this the only thing for us to do is to take you back to that girl."

The next day the giants set off by track with Silanting Kuning, on their way to Gumiloh's village. When half way there, they came to the house of an old woman called Grandmother Kilimayuh who often acted as guardian to children who were lost, looking after them until they grew up. She not only had the power of killing but also of giving life. That night they stayed in the house of Grandmother Kilimayuh.[1]

The next morning Grandmother Kilimayuh grabbed hold of Silanting Kuning and chopped him into pieces and put the pieces into a pot. She boiled the pot on her fire. The pieces which floated she skimmed off and threw away, for they were the ugly parts of Silanting Kuning. As soon as the remaining pieces were cooked they joined together to form a beautiful young man, so that Silanting Kuning emerged from the pot very handsome, with the previously bleached spots on his skin now appearing as gold, and with his hair all golden.

Then Grandmother Kilimayuh gave him a whole orang-utan skin, head and all, to wear as a coat. When Silanting Kuning got inside the skin, he looked just like an orang-utan. Grandfather Giant and Grandmother Giant then led him to a sugar-cane garden belonging to Gumiloh. In the garden he climbed up on the stump of a big tree, which had been cut off about fifteen feet from the ground, because at that height the trunk is not so thick and hard to chop through. There he sat, just like an orang-utan. The giants stayed beside the stream which ran along the edge of the sugar-cane garden.

While Silanting Kuning sat on the stump like an orang-utan, Grandmother Giant cut but one single stalk of sugar-cane. Immediately all the stalks of sugar-cane in the garden fell down also. Then Grandfather Giant pulled out but one single root of cassava and all the roots of cassava in the garden came up also. Then he pulled up but one single root of *keladi* and out came every root of *keladi* in the garden.[1]

That night Gumiloh dreamt that her sugar-cane garden was all destroyed by wild pigs. In the morning she told her two uncles,

[1] *Keladi* is an edible arum, apparently of the same species as the taro of the Pacific Islands.

Buku Tabu and Tungu Linau, who were her father's brothers, about her dream, and asked them to go to her sugar-cane garden to see what had happened. The uncles set off by boat. On and on downstream they went, until at last they came upon the giants sitting on the bank of the stream.

The giants' mouths were as big as the skylights in a longhouse,[1] their eyes were as big as the moon and their teeth were as big as fists. The uncles swung their canoe round in a panic.

They paddled back at full speed. But their boat was not fast enough for them, so they jumped out of it on to the track about a quarter of a mile below the landing-stage to run back towards their village. They tried to run too fast and fell over fainting. As soon as they could rise again, they dashed ahead so fast that they fell over once more. Time after time they ran and fell. When they did get to their longhouse, they raced up the steps so quickly that they toppled off them half way up. Time and time again they tried to climb the steps. At last they reached the top and the safety of their home.

Gumiloh thereupon went to another man called Sangau Labung, a man who was not a relative. She asked him to go to her sugar-cane garden to see what had happened. He said, "Why don't you ask your uncles?"

She replied, "I did ask them. And they went. But they met two big giants before they got there, and ran home frightened."

"Oh, nonsense," said Sangau Labung. "Tomorrow I will go myself and if I find any giants there, I will fight them."

In the evening Sangau Labung sharpened his fighting-knife. He said to his mother, "Mother, tomorrow morning get my breakfast ready very early, because I'm going to Gumiloh's sugar-cane garden. When I get there I may have to fight a giant."

He got up at daybreak. His mother said that the rice was not yet properly cooked, for it had not yet sucked up all the water in the pot.

"Never mind! Put it on my plate!" exclaimed Sangau Labung. He made her scoop it straight out of the pot on to his plate. With the steam still rising from it, he thrust a handful into his mouth.

"Goodness me, it's hot!" he gasped.

But he managed to gulp it all down. When he had finished he chewed a little betel and had a few puffs at a pipe. Then he set off downstream.

---

[1] Portions of the roof, perhaps as large as 12 ft x 10 ft, made so that they may be lifted to let in light.

Suddenly he came upon the giants. Back he shot, far faster than Gumiloh's uncles, so fast that he fell down and broke his nose. When at last he got up on to the outer verandah of the longhouse he fell down in a faint.

When Gumiloh saw Sangau Labung in a faint she ran to get a big hat to fan him with, so that he might come to consciousness again.

Gumiloh takes Silanting Kuning to her Village

The next morning Gumiloh herself accompanied by her two uncles set off for her sugar-cane garden. When their boat brought them in sight of the two giants sitting by the bank of the stream in the same place as on the day before, the uncles were once more very frightened, exclaiming to Gumiloh, "Look, see the giants!"

Gumiloh saw they were enormous. But she wanted to quieten the fears of her uncles, so she replied, "Nonsense, they're our grandfather and our grandmother."

At that moment Gumiloh noticed the orang-utan sitting on the top of the tree stump. Pointing to it, she said, "And that orang-utan there will be our pet."

They got out of their boat, and went up to the sugar-cane garden. When she set eyes on it, poor Gumiloh cried, "Oh shame! My whole garden has been destroyed by the giants!"

In despair she picked up one of the sugar-cane plants and propped it up in the earth. Immediately all the sugar-cane in the garden rose back into place, growing as before. Gumiloh then propped up a cassava root, and all the cassava roots grew up straight again. She did this with all the kinds of plants in her garden, and in a few moments the garden was completely restored.

By this time her uncles had become so angry at the destruction of poor Gumiloh's garden that they set upon the two giants. But every time one of the uncles aimed a blow at a giant, his arm swerved away and hit the other uncle instead. And every time the second uncle tried to hit a giant he hit the first uncle. The more the two uncles tried to fight the giants, the more they hurt each other.

Gumiloh did not like this fighting one bit. All the time she was trying very hard to stop the uncles from attacking the giants, calling to them, "Don't hit your grandmother and grandfather!"

Her words brought only a pause to their rage. They left the giants.

But then they attacked the orang-utan. The same thing happened as before, and they just hurt each other more.

At last Gumiloh rushed in between them. She herself caught hold of the orang-utan, tying it to herself with her long hair, so that she could lead it along. Then, with her hair as a lead, she led it along to the boat. The giants got in the boat also, although they had first to make themselves smaller to be able to do so. When they were all safely in the boat, they set off back to the village.

At the village, the orang-utan and the giants were put on the bottom platform of the young men's sleeping house, below the floor where the young men sleep. This made all the rest of the people in the village very angry with Gumiloh.

"What do you mean by bringing fearful giants and an orang-utan home with you?" they said. "What need have we of demons and apes in our village?"

The giants had become enormous again, now that they were out of the boat. When Sangau Labung saw them, he exclaimed, "Those are the giants which frightened me yesterday, and made me run home in terror, and faint when I got home."

All this time, Silanting Kuning, inside the orang-utan skin, was becoming furious at being left on this lower platform of the house. In his anger, he pulled up everything he could get hold of—the planks, the house poles, and anything else he could. He threw them down to the ground below. When Gumiloh saw his rage, she guessed the cause. So she took him up on to the top floor of the house in among all the young men who were there. The giants were left below.

Gumiloh's uncles told her to feed the orang-utan. She brought him a coconut shell containing rice mixed with a vegetable. When she gave it to him, he threw it to the ground. Gumiloh brought him more, this time on a plate, but not on her own plate. The orang-utan threw it also down to the ground.

The uncles said, "Perhaps the orang-utan does not want to eat off anything but your very own plate. Get your plate. Try giving him some rice and vegetable on it."

Gumiloh did as they told her. The orang-utan ate the food, the whole plateful.

But he was not yet satisfied. Once again he began to break up the floor of the room, throwing the pieces down to the ground. In this particular headhouse, there was a smaller loft above the main floor. It had been the sleeping place of Gumiloh's father before he married

Gumiloh's mother. Gumiloh took the orang-utan up into it. When he got up there, he gave no more trouble.

Gumiloh brought meals to the loft for two days. For these two days, Silanting Kuning, who was disguised as the orang-utan, did nothing except rest. But on the third day, he decided to try some of the medicines which the giants had given him earlier, and which he had not yet eaten. The first medicine which he tried was a medicine to make the day seem like night. As he ate the medicine, he sang the spell to make it work:

> *'Chuba ku ngasa urih sudi mandi,*
> *Berih akih ku antu Rigasih.*
> *Chuba ku ngasa ntama,*
> *Berih akih ku Antu Muta pirapa raya:*
> *Chilar chilar singkup pingan pijinak mata tidur;*
> *Urih kura rinda kura panchir pingawa.*
>
> . . . .
>
> *Anak biyak jangan nangis!*
> *Orang tua jangan batok!*
> *Manok jangan bangkukok!*
> *Babi jangan bangkuwek!*
> *Kuching jangang mangaong!*
> *Asuh jangang bangkaong!*
> *Orang nutok tidur di luar!*
> *Orang pegi chari pakuh chari*
> *Rebung tidur di utan!*
> *Orang pegi mara–uh*
> *Tidur pangkalan!'*

'Let me try this medicine, so strong, so potent,
Given to me by the giant, Rigasih.[1]
Let me test these magical things,
Given to me by the Seven-headed Giant from the vast swamp:
Glittering pieces of plate to drowse the eyes;
Medicine of tortoise-shell, powerful medicine from the small tortoise.

. . . .

> Babies must not cry!
> Old people must not cough!
> Fowls must not cackle!
> Pigs must not squeal!

---

[1] The proper name of the giant whom Silanting Kuning first met.

Cats must not caterwaul!
Dogs must not whine!
Pounders of paddy must fall asleep out-doors!
Gatherers of fern and shoots of bamboo[1]
Must drop to sleep in the countryside!
Persons busy about their boats
Must fall asleep at the landing-place!'

As the song ended, day began to change into night.

When it was fully dark, and everybody in the village had fallen asleep, Silanting Kuning opened up his orang-utan skin, and climbed out of it. He went down to the stream, bathed, and returned to the headhouse. Then he got inside his orang-utan skin again. As soon as he did so, the darkness gave way to sunlight. All who had fallen down asleep awoke. There was great wonder as to what had happened. The people said to one another, "The sun must have fallen sick."

Then all took up their work just as they had left off. Those who had been pounding paddy began to pound again. Those who had been gathering edible fern or bamboo shoots went on gathering or set off for home. Those who had fallen asleep at the landing-stage busied themselves about their boats again.

Silanting Kuning Makes Love to Gumiloh's Sister

The day began to grow dark once more with the ordinary coming of night.

Silanting Kuning again opened up his orang-utan coat. He wished to visit Gumiloh. But he could not go straight to her, because she had agreed to marry a Malay, called Bilantur. Instead he visited Gumiloh's younger sister, Kumang Malidi. Unlike lovers nowadays he did not sneak into her house. He boldly called upon her servant to open the door. He sang a song:

'O am induh inang![2]
Buka kanching lawang dinding
Ngundang tunang ku udah bujang;
Ngundang ayam ku di angkuh.'

[1] Common Land Dayak foods.

[2] The translation of this word is difficult. Clearly the girl was a servant of some kind, but of what status it is impossible to say. The Land Dayaks do not have servants, and the allusion here suggests a Malay, or other, origin for this part of the story. The allusion could, however, be easily understood by the Land Dayaks. In the first place, they know

'O, dear maid-servant!
Open up the door,
Open wide the door.
For me to see my Love, a full-grown maid;
For me to visit her whom I now claim.'

The maid-servant answered, singing:

'*Ndah mah ku mau*
Muka kanching lawang dinding,
Muka pintu lawang dora!
Takut ku Minyawai Siludai Ali!
Takut nubah nungkal binua kami!
Minyawai tuh sigih bisumpai
Rarai bigalang rundut!
Takut nubah manok nyarang babi,
Mantang binua kalimon ari!'

'I have no wish at all
To open up the door,
To open wide the door!
I fear it's Minyawai Siludai Ali!
I fear he comes to slay us all!
Minyawai with tangled hair
In curls all over his body!
I fear he'll kill the fowls, slay all the pigs,
Destroy the village in a time of peace!'

Silanting Kuning sang in answer:

'*O am induh inang!*
Bukai aku tuh Minyawai
Bisumpai rarai bigalong rundut!
Bilantur mah nama aku!
Gigi ku berkikir,
Pala ku bukukur!'

of status differentiations observed by other cultural groups in Borneo. Secondly, some households have attached persons who do not belong to them by birth. Since such persons join the households of their own free will to suit their convenience—they may, for instance, be widows—they do not have an inferior status in the community at large. But they have slightly less choice than full members as to the work they do for the household in return for their keep. They are in fact never truly servants, but their position may make it easier for listeners to this tale to imagine a state of society in which such persons would be complaisant enough to wait upon them.

'O, dear maid-servant!
I'm not that Minyawai
With hair in curls all over my body!
Bilantur is the name of me!
My teeth are filed,
My head is shaved!'

The maid-servant said, "If you are really Bilantur, where is your boat?"

Silanting Kuning answered, "My boat is downstream from the landing-stage."

"What is the sign of your boat?" asked the maid-servant.

Silanting Kuning sang:

'*Rangkang ngah ugah kayu ulah ulah,*
Ya mah tanda prauh aku mang juah.'

'From bushes near the bank twigs tremble in the stream,
That's the sign my boat is coming soon.'[1]

But the maid-servant said, "Even though that is true, I am still frightened to open the door, in case you do turn out to be Minyawai."

Silanting Kuning sang in reply:

'*Antih ndah kita mau*
Muka kanching lawang dinding,
Muka pintu lawang dora.'

'They have no wish
To open up the door,
To open wide the door.'

He then went over to a nearby jackfruit tree. As he climbed it, and from it on to the other palms as he mentioned them, he sang:

'*Silalai nangkak rinda nyampah atuh buntan gading;*
Silalai buntan gading nyampah atuh pinang;
Silalai pinang giring nyampah ra pangong
Adi ku dayang Kumang Malidi pangau gantong.
Lamunyih saduh ayun.'

[1] I am not sure of the translation here. It may be that the reference is to some kind of symbol of the boat, but, if so, I cannot explain the meaning. Raseh himself seemed to be in doubt as to what was meant.

'The bending jackfruit tree curves down to the yellow coconut palm;[1]
The bending yellow palm curves down to the areca palm;
The bending areca palm curves down above the bed
Of my young kinsmaiden, Kumang Malidi, up in the loft.[2]
This ends my song.'

As Silanting Kuning finished singing, the areca palm bent down beneath the roof of the loft where Kumang Malidi was sleeping. Awoken by the noise, Kumang Malidi sang:

'*Ah doh akai adoh indai!*
Sapa dama anak tamuwai,
Ngunchang nguyang pangong aku!
Sangkah ku ribut.
Hari toh ndah ribut!
Sangkah ku ujan.
Hari toh ndah ujan!
Sangkah ku kayu patah.
Ndah dekat kampong!
Sangkah ku kayu rabah.
Ndah dekat rurung!
Sangkah ku batuh bibaring.
Ndah dekat gunong!'

'Oh dear! Oh mother dear!
Who is this being, so strange,
Shaking and tossing my bed!
I think it is the wind.
But it is not a windy day!
I think it is the rain.
But it is not a rainy day!
I think it is a broken branch.
But none are near the homes!
I think it is a fallen tree.
But groves are not so close!
I think it is a rolling stone.
But no, the peak is not so near!'

[1] Two species of coconut palm are grown by the Land Dayaks. The one referred to here has a yellow tinge to its trunk distinguishing it from the commoner species.

[2] Today at least, Land Dayak girls do not sleep in lofts. On the other hand, Sea Dayak girls do. There may, therefore, be a Sea Dayak origin to this particular part of the story. Raseh, however, was of the opinion that this was a past practice of Land Dayaks.

Silanting Kuning then decided to try another of the medicines given him by the giants. This medicine could turn him into a scorpion or a centipede. As he held the medicine, he sang:

> '*Chuba ku ngasa urih ku sidi mandi,*
> *Ntama ku bisa sibarang bisa,*
> *Jadi kala lalipan mah ku maoh!*'

> 'Let me try my medicine intense and strong,
> My powerful medicine of wondrous power,
> Which can make a scorpion or a centipede be my disguise!'

As he ended his song, he changed into a centipede. He crawled through the roof, and fell down right on to Kumang Malidi's chest, as she lay stretched out on her bed. Quickly she brushed him off, and he fell to the ground with a thud. Immediately he was transformed back into the handsome person of Silanting Kuning. Kumang Malidi did not see the change occur. Knowing someone was there, she sang out:

> '*O am induh inang!*
> *Pantau biliyau dama majau!*
> *Tiup api damar mura!*
> *Ngantah ngilala anak timuwai toh,*
> *Bagus gilah rambut panjai saribu dapah,*
> *Tubuh nya basai tujuh satah,*
> *Mata nya mirah rupa giranang lalah.*'

> 'O, dear maid-servant!
> Light up the torch of majau gum!
> Blow up the gum into a glow!
> For us to gaze upon this person from afar,
> Of shining beauty with his hair a thousand arm-spans long,
> His body seven forearms tall,
> His eyes as red as paint fresh mixed from powder.[1]

Silanting Kuning thereupon sang out:

> '*O am induh inang!*
> *Ndah usah mantan bilayau damar majau!*
> *Ndah usah tiup api damar mura!*

---

[1] Chinese traders sell a kind of red paint in the form of lumps of powder. It is much desired by the Dayaks for colouring baskets, rattan girdles, small bamboo containers for the roasted and powdered snail shell they chew with their areca-nut, and for festival hats and other articles.

Bukai aku Minyawai Siludai Ali.
Silanting Kuning mah nama aku.
Pala ku bukukur gigi ku berkikir,
Ya mah tanda aku!
Rangkang ulah ulah kayu ngah ugah,
Yah mah tanda aku mang juah!'

'O, dear maid-servant!
There is no need to light the torch of majau gum!
There is no need to blow the gum into a glow!
I am not Minyawai Siludai Ali.
Silanting Kuning is the name I bear.
My head all shaved, my teeth sharp filed,
That's the sign of me!
And trembling twigs from trees beside the stream,
That's the sign I'm coming by!'

The maid-servant blew up the fire and brought a torch of majau gum to the sleeping-place of her mistress. Kumang Malidi then beheld a most beautiful man standing near her bed. As soon as she saw him, she sang:

'*O am induh inang!*
Masak padi chi padi nanyi padi pulut!
Paluntan mutong manok jagau jawa.'

'O, dear maid-servant!
Cook up a meal of rice, white rice, make ready *pulit* rice!
Kill for the pot a cock of largest kind!'

Silanting Kuning sang to the servant:

'*O am induh inang!*
Anang masak priok kachil!
Priok basai buah tuba!
Situan ku ndah makai!
Sibulan ku ndah majuh!'

'O, dear maid-servant!
Don't cook a tiny pot!
A pot the size of a derris-fruit!
For one whole year I've not had a meal!
For one whole month I've not had a bite!'

When the rice and fowl were cooked, the servant brought them to Kumang Malidi and Silanting Kuning, and they ate their fill together.

When they had finished their large meal, Kumang Malidi had a sleeping-mat brought and arranged a bed for Silanting Kuning on the far side of the room from her own bed. She then lay down to sleep, and Silanting Kuning lay down on his bed also. But as soon as the fire had died right down, his desire to seduce Kumang Malidi moved him.

He rose from his mat, and crept across to her bed. When he reached it, he felt for her with his hand. He found that she was sleeping on her side. Kumang Malidi felt his hand moving over her, and became angry. Silanting Kuning was not put off. He teased her, singing:

> '*Tidu ngilantu bangun ngaluda!*
> *Rupa bangkai orang gila.*
> *Tidu ngilantu bangun ngiriding!*
> *Rupa bangkai mayang panging.*
> *Tidu ngilantu bangun ngaludang!*
> *Rupa bangkai mayang tumbang.*'

> 'Sleeping so deeply, get up smartly!
> Your body's like the corpse of one gone mad.
> Sleeping so deeply, rise up sideways!
> Your body's like a fallen sago palm.
> Sleeping so deeply, jump to your feet!
> Your body's like a sago log.'

Kumang Malidi turned over on to her back. She then sang out to her maid-servant:

> '*O am induh inang!*
> *Asa kina pangkah tandok rusah oleh nawah!*
> *Asa kina pangkong tandok jungong oleh nawah!*
> *Pulau sulong inyam patik rangkang tuang!*
> *Inyam patuk anyau bangau sabung ranchang!*
> *O am induh inang asa ni induh inang?*'

> 'O, dear maid-servant!
> I feel as though struck by the horn of a deer wounded in the hunt!
> I feel as though struck by the horn of a mouse wounded in the hunt!

I feel as though brushed by the twigs in a forest patch in the fields!

I feel as though pecked by the beak of the cock waved o'er the young![1]

Oh how, my dear maiden, do you find it then, my maid-servant dear?'

The maid-servant exclaimed, "Oh, he is not a good man! He says his name is Silanting Kuning, but I am sure he has been a very bad man under another name." She then replied to Kumang Malidi by singing:

> '*Asa katipak asa katipau,*
> *Bunyi laut laut bipulah;*
> *Bunyi singanan bipulah rambing!*'

> 'It is like a rumble, like a roar,
> The sound of the sea, the raging sea;
> The clangour of Malays making boats!'

Silanting Kuning now sang:

> '*O am dih dayung dara Kumang Malidi!*
> *Ndah mah minta banyak minta sidikit!*
> *Satampah daun padi sikilan duan jari!*'

> 'O, my dear maiden, Kumang Malidi!
> I do not ask for very much, I ask for but a tiny bit!
> The width of a paddy-leaf, the space between two fingers opened out!'

Kumang Malidi then yielded to him. They stayed together for the rest of the night.

Just before dawn, Silanting Kuning left her room to return to the headhouse. When he reached there, he put on his orang-utan skin, and kept it on throughout the day.

---

[1] The reference is to the festival held for an infant sometime after its birth. The priest of the ancestral cult waves a white cock over the infant as he expresses the blessings which he hopes will attend it.

PLATE VII

Rari, a maiden from Mayang, returns to her village after a festival with her share of the food which has been offered to the spirits—rice in the basket and cooked *pulit* rice in bamboo containers.

Gumiloh Seeks the Culprit and Succumbs Herself

In the morning, Kumang Malidi told her elder sister, Gumiloh, how a stranger had come in the night to make love to her. Gumiloh decided she should call a village meeting to try to find out who it was who had gone to her young sister, Kumang Malidi, in such a way. In the evening, she struck the big gongs to summon everyone to the meeting. As she did so, she sang:

'Deng dong ku mangkong!
Bandai birintai sanang daong!
Ngilamung puchuk nangkah turun!
Dih, Patu, Laja, Kaleng, Sangkeng,
Sangau Labung, Pai Abang dari pancha,
Ramiya Ganduh balai gantung!
Ada pengukum pengaum aku malam tuh!'

'Ding-dong, I strike the gongs!
Struck in a line, they sound "sanang-daong"!
The sound out-tops the jackfruit trees in the countryside!
Come here, Patu, Laja, Kaleng, Sangkeng,
Sangau Labung and Pai Abang, from the house for men,
From out of the headhouse, from the bachelors' home![1]
For there is a fine to be fixed by me this night!'

All the men in the village came along to the meeting, which was held in Gumiloh's house.

Pai Abang asked Gumiloh, "What is the meaning of this meeting?"

"I am not going to mince words," said Gumiloh. "I am going to speak out. I want to know if you have with you in your bachelors' house any visitors who might have gone to seduce Kumang Malidi in the night. Or was it one of you?"

They all denied that they had intruded on Kumang Malidi during the night, as she lay on her bed. They said, too, that there was no stranger in their bachelors' house. More than one remarked, however, "Of course, we have your pet orang-utan with us!"

[1] All synonyms for the one building.

PLATE VIII

Preparing for a festival. The women make ready bamboo containers in which to cook delicacies, while men bring more bamboo for containers and for making the platform for the offerings.

I

The meeting could find out nothing. When no one had anything more to say, it broke up. The young men went back to the headhouse and settled down to sleep until the morning. After daybreak everyone went out to work as usual and nothing extraordinary happened until midday.

At midday, Silanting Kuning wished to go visiting again. He sang his song to make the day as dark as night. As he ended his song, darkness came over the noonday sun. Everyone fell asleep in the places where they were working. Silanting Kuning got out of his orang-utan skin, and set out once more—this time to visit his real love, Gumiloh.

Once again he first of all climbed the jackfruit tree, and from the jackfruit tree went on to the yellow coconut palm, and from the yellow coconut palm on to the areca palm, and from the areca palm down on to the roof of Gumiloh's house. Again he changed himself into a centipede, and dropped right on to Gumiloh's breast. She brushed him quickly off on to the floor. He landed with a thud and was immediately transformed back into his own handsome figure. Then the same things happened as had happened when he was with Kumang Malidi. He sang to Gumiloh as he had sung to her, and Gumiloh answered him as Kumang Malidi had done.

Gumiloh yielded to him, and they lay together until the next day was just about to dawn. Then Silanting Kuning knew it was time for him to return to the bachelors' house, so he sang:

'*Pa siang hari pagi pigasak!*
Di malaka ulu tipayan!
Nyuruh tubu ku riga riga,
Rupa baka burung Raya,
Gilang gilih rupa pasandong,
Sangar ngaso ulu tipayan.
Manok kukoh mada hari taweh siang!'

'The day is near, the morning dawns!
Don't hold me from the bathing-place!
Let my body glisten like
The body of the Raya bird,
With glinting feathers all agleam,
Parading round the bathing-place.
The crowing cocks tell of the day!'[1]

---

[1] This is a particularly difficult song to translate. If the translation is free, it is so because it is unconstrained by an understanding of all the words.

But Gumiloh would not let him go. In order to escape, he sang:

'*Chuba ku ninyam kala,*
Lalipan ninyam tadung langangan!'

'I try to be changed into a scorpion,
Or a centipede, or into a big king-cobra!'

As his song ended, he became a centipede. Gumiloh grabbed it, but it leapt out of her hand, and became Silanting Kuning again. She grabbed again, and managed to catch hold of the back of his loin-cloth. He tore himself free, ran quickly back to the headhouse, and got inside his orang-utan skin. But he left behind a little piece of his loin-cloth in Gumiloh's hand.

Silanting Kuning Visits the Dragon-chief

Later in the morning, Silanting Kuning, still disguised as an orang-utan, asked Gumiloh's uncles for a throwing-net, saying he wished to go fishing. The uncles said that he could go fishing with them.

The uncles and the orang-utan set out down the river, using a small canoe, and not taking any food because they intended to return that evening. They went downstream until they came to a deep pool. The orang-utan wished to cast his net there. The uncles said, "You cannot cast your net here. It is a forbidden pool. No one may fish here."

The orang-utan did not take the slightest notice of what they said. He immediately cast his net into the forbidden pool.

The net sank right down through the pool and caught on the top of the roof of a house. This was the house of Singiyang Naga. He was the chief of a people who lived beneath the pool, where there was another countryside, just like the countryside of Mentu Tapuh.

The people who lived in this country beneath the pool were very pretty and handsome. But they could also change themselves into dragons. They could be one thing or the other—either people or fearful dragons. They also had a rule that any human beings who went down to the bottom of the pool had to be killed. They must never be allowed to return to the earth.

When he felt his net caught on the roof of the house of the Dragon-chief, Silanting Kuning, still disguised as the orang-utan, went forward to Buku Tabu, one of the uncles of Gumiloh, and kicked him.

Immediately, Buku Tabu was changed into a stalk of sugar-cane, growing out of the bow of the canoe. He next went to the other end of the canoe and kicked Tungu Linau, the other uncle of Gumiloh. Immediately, he was changed into a wild-sago palm, growing out of the stern of the canoe.

Silanting Kuning took off his orang-utan skin. Then he dived down through the pool to the forbidden land beneath it.

When he reached the bottom he was in front of the house of Singiyang Naga, the Dragon-chief. He called out to the Dragon-chief to ask whether he might come up into his house.

The Dragon-chief answered, "Yes, you are welcome. Just hold on a moment while I put steps down for you to come up."

The Dragon-chief then lowered steps of which each single step was a knife-blade turned on edge.

When Silanting Kuning saw the steps, he knew he could not get up them without help. He asked a cock to lead him up. But the cock replied, "Goodness me, no! Even a fly settling on those blades gets cut to pieces."

At this moment the Dragon-chief appeared at the doorway of his house. He called down to Silanting Kuning, "Wait a minute! I've got something for you."

He drew his spear from its scabbard. It was a spear as wide as a banana frond. He raised it above his head. Then with all his might he threw it down at Silanting Kuning.

The spear missed Silanting Kuning. It passed right between his legs, ripping the tail of his loin-cloth to pieces.

Seizing the spear, Silanting Kuning cried out, "On guard, Grandfather!" and then heaved the spear with tremendous force back at him.

Missing the Dragon-chief, the spear travelled the whole length of his longhouse, passed right through the end wall, and, falling to the ground below where a man was feeding a big pig, the point pierced the pig, killing it, and the handle struck the man, killing him also.

Silanting Kuning then asked a firefly to lead him up the steps of blades. The firefly told him, "Wherever I step, there you must step also."

He did as the firefly had directed, stepping exactly on the places where the firefly settled. And so they mounted the steps, and came into the house of the Dragon-chief.

In proper fashion, the Dragon-chief spread mats to receive him hospitably. But although he made it look like a good welcome, he had in fact spread poison on the mats to turn his guest into ashes. Silanting Kuning, however, did not sit on the mats spread so temptingly for him. Instead, he sat on the floor.

The Dragon-chief asked, "Why do you not sit on the mats?"

Silanting Kuning answered, "Oh, I feel too hot. I would much rather sit on the floor. It's cooler."

"You are wise," said the Dragon-chief, taking the poison off the mats. Silanting Kuning then sat upon them.

The Dragon-chief brought two enormous wine bowls. The wine they had in them was not true wine. It was the blood of human beings who had dived into the pool. One bowl was for the Dragon-chief himself, and the other was for Silanting Kuning. The Dragon-chief began to drink first. When he tipped his head back to swallow the blood, Silanting Kuning struck him on his Adam's apple. Then, as he was blindly spluttering out the blood he had swallowed, Silanting Kuning poured his bowlful through the floor slats down on to the ground below. When the Dragon-chief recovered, he told him that he had drunk it.

Silanting Kuning Outwits the Dragon-chief

The wife of the Dragon-chief killed a fowl, and cooked it, cooking rice also. When the meal was ready, they ate it. By the time they had finished, it was getting dark. The Dragon-chief said to Silanting Kuning, "Where are you going to sleep?"

"Oh, on the inner verandah, I suppose," he replied. He then asked for a gourd of water, a mosquito-net, and a basket-work fish-trap. He said he needed the gourd of water in case he should want to relieve himself during the night and therefore require the water to wash himself afterwards, and that he needed the fish-trap in order to have something to which he could tie his mosquito-net. The Dragon-chief brought him the three things to the place on the inner verandah where he was going to sleep. The Dragon-chief then went back into his room.

As soon as the Dragon-chief was out of sight, Silanting Kuning placed the fish-trap beneath his bed-covering, and put the gourd at the top of it, so that it would seem like his head. He intended to go up into the loft above the verandah to sleep.

Just as he was about to go up into the loft, the Dragon-chief called out, "Are you asleep, my grandson?"

"No. Not yet, Grandfather," answered Silanting Kuning, "because my head is spinning with all that wine you gave me."

After he was in the loft, the Dragon-chief called again. Silanting Kuning did not answer. Three times the Dragon-chief called, but each time he got no answer. "Ah!" muttered the Dragon-chief to himself. "Good! Now my new grandson is asleep. This time he will die."

He took up his great fighting-knife, a fathom long, called *Dong Daong Jamau Rampang*, and went out to the place where he believed Silanting Kuning was sleeping. He smote a fierce blow at the head of the bed, slicing through the mosquito-net and right through the gourd. When the gourd was cut, the water in it poured out down to the ground below. As he heard it falling, the Dragon-chief exclaimed, "Ah! Now he is slain." Then he got down on his knees to lap up such water as was left on the floor, believing it to be the blood of Silanting Kuning.

He then hurried back into his room to blow up his fire to light a torch in order that he might see more clearly the body of the boy whom he had slain. Up in the loft where Silanting Kuning was, there was a cat. Silanting Kuning said to it, "Please go along and urinate through the ceiling on to the Dragon-chief's fire." The cat did as it was asked. Whenever the Dragon-chief managed to get a glow into his fire, the cat put it out.

While the Dragon-chief was struggling to get his torch alight, Silanting Kuning hastened down from the loft and, throwing away the fish-trap and the remains of the gourd, got into the bed himself.

He had just got himself settled, when the Dragon-chief succeeded in getting his torch alight. He came with it towards the bed. When he was very near, Silanting Kuning spoke, "What are you looking for, Grandfather?"

"Goodness me!" exclaimed the Dragon-chief. "I thought you were dead. What wonderful luck you must have! With such luck, it is certain that you will become very rich. And you will succeed in winning Gumiloh as your wife. But to do so, you must first kill Bilantur, the Malay whom she has agreed to marry."

The Dragon-chief then invited Silanting Kuning into his room to sleep with his granddaughter, Dayang Silujah, a very lovely girl.

While he was lying with Dayang Silujah, he asked her, "What is your grandfather's most potent medicine?"

She replied, "A fighting-knife with a chip out of the middle of the blade, a bottle with a broken top, the shell of a small tortoise, and a little bottle of life-giving elixir which he keeps in his mouth. This little bottle you must take first. Seize it when we get up in the morning, while grandfather is yawning."

Early in the morning, when the Dragon-chief was yawning just after getting up, Silanting Kuning grabbed the bottle out of his mouth. The Dragon-chief exclaimed, "Ah! Now you have got that you will become the richest and bravest man on earth."

They all had breakfast together.

When it was well on into the morning, the Dragon-chief asked Silanting Kuning, "What else do you want from me, Grandson?"

"I want from you, Grandfather," answered Silanting Kuning, "a knife with a chipped blade, a bottle with a broken top, and a shell of the small species of tortoise."

"Oh, dear!" said the Dragon-chief, "if I give you all that, I shall have absolutely no medicine left. All will be gone." But he gave him the lot.

The granddaughter of the Dragon-chief, Dayang Silujah, then caught many fowls, about a thousand, one whole boat-load. These she gave to Silanting Kuning.

"When are you going to return home?" asked the Dragon-chief.

"Today," replied Silanting Kuning, "but I wish to go back through the old jungle, as the young jungle would cut my legs too much." These words meant that he wished to go up through the deep pool. But he said them only to deceive the Dragon-chief, because he really intended to return through the shallow water above the pool.

When the Dragon-chief heard his answer, he walked out of sight, changed himself into a big dragon, and went to the deep pool, so as to catch and eat Silanting Kuning as he passed through. But Silanting Kuning went through the shallow water, where the dragon was frightened to chase him.

Silanting Kuning reached his boat and got back into his orang-utan skin. He kicked the sugar-cane stalk and it changed back into one of the uncles of Gumiloh. Then he kicked the wild-sago palm and it changed back into the other uncle of Gumiloh. The uncles exclaimed, "Goodness, we've been in such a deep sleep!" The fowls which the granddaughter of the Dragon-chief had given him had changed into fish, so that the boat was now full of fish.

Silanting Kuning said to the uncles, "When we get back to the village, if anyone asks for a fish you must give him two. If he asks for two, you must give him three. If he asks for four, you must give him five. You must always give everyone one more than they ask for."

They arrived at the landing-place in Gumiloh's village. The uncles did as they had been told, and everybody in the village received a great lot of fish, enough for each person to make one jarful of preserved fish. The uncles of Gumiloh got enough to make two jarsful each.[1]

Gumiloh said, "Ah, my uncles! When you have the orang-utan with you, you can get plenty of fish. When you are alone, you never have such luck. It is the luck of the orang-utan which has helped you today."

"No!" said the uncles. "That has nothing whatever to do with it. We had bad luck when we were young. Now that we are grown-up, even getting a little elderly, we have very good luck. The moon has a lot to do with it too. It is now full moon. We always have good luck at the full moon."

Gumiloh Weds Bilantur

After the fish had been shared out amongst the people, Pai Abang said to Gumiloh, "You must call a meeting tonight to arrange for your marriage to Bilantur."

In the evening the meeting took place, and the plans were made. The next morning a party from the village set off to fetch Gumiloh's betrothed. As he was a Malay, he lived downstream nearer the coast. When the party reached Bilantur's house, they told his father that they wanted to take Bilantur back to their village to marry Gumiloh. He agreed to the match; Bilantur's mother agreed also. The party stayed the night in the house of Bilantur's mother and father.

In the morning Bilantur loaded all his belongings into his boat, which was made all of brass, and set out with the party for Gumiloh's village. It was evening when they reached it. Bilantur stayed on the verandah outside Gumiloh's house. Gumiloh cooked a meal of fowl and rice, and took it to him. She did not cook him pork because he was a Malay.

When everyone had eaten, Gumiloh's uncles went around the village

[1] The fish are preserved, usually so that they may be kept to be used later as a festival delicacy, by being put raw in a jar together with cooked rice and salt.

inviting her relatives to come to the gathering in her house to witness her marriage to Bilantur. When all those who cared to come had gathered in the house, one of the old men said that henceforth the couple were to be husband and wife. Other elderly men spoke, giving them advice as to how they should care for one another, how they should quarrel only when alone in their own home, and so on. In this way, Bilantur became the husband of Gumiloh. When the gathering had broken up, he lay down with her under her mosquito-net.

In the meantime Silanting Kuning had sought the help of a scorpion, which now carried out his plan. The scorpion went to the bed, and before Bilantur could make love to Gumiloh it stung his penis, making it impossible for him to do so. In the morning Silanting Kuning sent a paping insect to lick it better. But in the evening he sent a mosquito to bite it again. Each morning and each night Bilantur received this treatment, so that although he was often about to make love to Gumiloh he always failed at the last moment.

A few days after his wedding, Bilantur called a meeting to arrange for an expedition against Minyawai, to avenge the death of Gumiloh's father. It was agreed at the meeting that the next day all should work making war-canoes. In the morning the men set out to fell the trees. Bilantur cut down a *piruntan* tree. By evening many boats had been made. After the workers had returned to the village, another meeting was held to plan the expedition.

The next morning a war-party set out, with Bilantur as the leader.

Silanting Kuning makes his War-canoe

When the meeting had decided to make canoes, Silanting Kuning made up his mind to make himself the finest war-canoe of all. Still disguised as an orang-utan, he asked the uncles of Gumiloh for an axe, a big knife, and a plane. He also asked for a large basket of rice, a basket which held twenty-four gallons. Then he and the uncles set off upstream to fell the tree to make their canoe. As soon as they were out of sight of the village, Silanting Kuning took off his orang-utan skin.

In the jungle, they made a hut. They cooked food, ate it, and by then it was dark. They slept all night. In the morning they had break-fast, and then went to find a suitable tree. Silanting Kuning picked out a *para* tree. He sang to it:

'O batang Para!
Biawan nantih mau kita pake,
Pake ku prauh ngayau,
Ruwang nya pake ku
Pingandung ayer darah,
Mutus budi mawang buleng malas
Mah bapa dayang dara Gumiloh?
Pangau gantung lamunyih saduh ayun.'

'O, Para trunk!
Do you wish to be used,
To be used as my war-canoe,
Your inside to be used by me
To hold blood,
To repay the death, to avenge the slaying
Of the father and mother of Gumiloh?
This is the end of my song.'

The *para* tree sang in answer:

'O am samih!
Ndah mah ku mau pake kita prauh ngayau.
Ruwang ku nadai kala ngandung ayer darah.
Pake kita pegi nuba, pegi nyala,
Pegi machat mah ku mau.'

'O, dear friend!
I do not want to be used as your war-canoe.
My inside has never held blood.
I want only to be a canoe for fishing with poison, for fishing with
    a throwing-net,
For fishing with a drag-net.'

Silanting Kuning was angry. He slashed at the tree. The tree cried.
So he left it.

He went higher up the hill, until he came to a tree of the kind known
as *kiladan banang*. He sang to this tree as he had sung to the *para* tree.
The tree sang in reply:

'O am samih!
Mau mah ku pake prauh ngayau.
Ruwang ku pake pingandung ayer darah.'

'O, dear friend!
I wish to be used as a war-canoe.
I want my inside to hold blood.'

Silanting Kuning sang to it:

'O am Kiladan Banang!
Angkat nigal minari,
Angkat manchah dibu langi,
Duloh ngadah kapala Minyawai Siludai Ali,
Nubah nungkal binua kami,
Nubah manok, nyarang babi,
Mantang binua limon ari.'

'O, dear Kiladan Banang!
Rise up to dance,
Rise, clap, and spread your arms,
As the first to welcome the head of Minyawai Siludai Ali,
Who raided our village,
Who stole our fowls, who slaughtered our pigs,
Who destroyed our village in a time of peace.'

The *kiladan banang* tree danced. When it had finished its dance Silanting Kuning chopped it down.

Silanting Kuning then called to him all the animals of the jungle. From many parts of the forest they came—bears, *sambhur* deer, barking-deer, mouse-deer, orang-utans, gibbons, black monkeys, argus pheasants, *bubot* birds, and all the insects which eat into wood. The insects and the large animals bit out the wood from the trunk to hollow it into a canoe—all except the mouse-deer, who acted as watchmen while the other animals worked. When the canoe was fully shaped, the argus pheasants painted the sides in the many-coloured designs of their own feathers. The bright red-and-black *bubot* birds painted the ends. They painted the bow in red and the stern in black. When all the work was done, the bears and the orang-utans dragged the canoe down to the stream.

The uncles of Gumiloh had not gone with Silanting Kuning into the forest. They had stayed back at the hut to cook the great basketful of rice. This kept them so busy that they knew nothing about the work that was being done on the canoe. When they beheld it on the river, finished, they were overcome with surprise. "What a beautiful canoe!" they exclaimed.

When the meal was ready, Silanting Kuning invited all the animals to share in it. They ate their fill. Then they went on their separate ways. Silanting Kuning and Gumiloh's uncles set off for the village.

Before they reached the village, Silanting Kuning changed himself back into an orang-utan. As he did so, the uncles forgot about his ever having appeared as a man. When they arrived at the village landing-stage, he went straight to his place in the headhouse.

The Obstacles on the River

In the evening Silanting Kuning asked Gumiloh's uncles to arrange supplies for himself and a party to follow Bilantur on the war-expedition against Minyawai. He asked Gumiloh to make a coloured basket to hold Minyawai's head.

He also asked for eggs to be brought to him, in the same number as there were to be men in his party. He said words over these eggs. Then he gave one egg to each man, and kept one for himself. He said that each man should crush his egg in his hands to break the shell. A chicken would come from each. If the chicken were a female, it would prove that the man holding that egg was faint-hearted. If the chicken were a male, it would mean that the holder of the egg was brave. Everyone broke his egg. From all of them came female chickens, except from that of Silanting Kuning. From his egg a cock sprang out and crowed lustily in the midst of the gathering.

In the morning the supplies were loaded into the war-canoe, and the party set out after Bilantur's party. Silanting Kuning took off his orang-utan skin. At last his party overtook Bilantur and his men at a place where they were held up by a great mass of logs milling up and down in the water in front of them.

Bilantur called out, "If any man can stop these logs milling up and down in front of us, he shall become the husband of Gumiloh!"

"How can that be?" exclaimed Silanting Kuning. "Surely Gumiloh has already become your wife.[1]

"Have you tried your medicine on these logs?" he added.

"Yes," said Bilantur, "but it will not stop them."

"Have you tried singing to the logs?"

"Yes, but it will not stop them."

"Try again."

So Bilantur sang:

[1] A taunt. She was, of course, already wed, but hardly married. Presumably, Bilantur had given up in despair.

'O am Batang timbul tingalam!
Nantih mah Batang timbul tingalam!
Nantih bala Patu biribu,
Nantih Laja laksa,
Melebat daun tapang raya.'

'O, Logs, thrusting around!
Pause, Logs, in your milling about!
Pause for Patu's warriors a thousand strong,
Pause for the party of Laja, a million strong,
As many as the leaves on a huge honey-tree.'

The logs kept on moving about.
Silanting Kuning then sang to them:

'O am Batang timbul tingalam!
Nantih mah Batang timbul tingalam!
Nantih bala ku biribu,
Nantih gumba ku laksa,
Ndah tiriken jarum China,
Sakulak langah mampah
Ndah tiriken antu duah.'

'O, Logs thrusting around!
Pause, Logs, in your milling about!
Pause for my party a thousand strong,
Pause for my million giants,
As countless as Chinese needles,[1]
As many as a coconut-shellful of sunflower seeds,
Too many to be counted by a couple of demons.'

As he ended his song, the logs sank to the bottom of the river, allowing the whole war-party to go forward. As they went upstream, Silanting Kuning always brought up the rear.

After rounding several more points on the river, the leaders of the party found their way blocked once more. Clumps of bamboo of the *singiyang* species were shooting their canes, like spears, at great speed across the river. The party dare not pass. Bilantur sang to the spears as he had sung to the logs, but they kept on shooting across the water.

Silanting Kuning came up. Bilantur said to him, "Once again we

---

[1] Apparently the sewing needles sold by Chinese in the bazaar. Although the Land Dayaks themselves work iron to make knives and larger implements, the quantity, quality and cheapness of these needles excite their admiration.

can do nothing. You try, and if you or anyone else can succeed, whoever it be shall become the husband of Gumiloh." So Silanting Kuning sang to the *singiyang* bamboo as he had sung to the logs. As soon as he ended his song, no more canes shot across the river.

Now all this time Bilantur was under the impression that the obstacles which the party had met had been placed in their path by the device of Minyawai. Actually they were arranged by Singiyang Naga the Dragon-chief, whom Silanting Kuning had visited beneath the pool, when he had gone fishing with Gumiloh's uncles. During that visit, he had been taught the songs which he now sang by the Dragon-chief. When the Dragon-chief heard the songs, he stopped the logs and the spears and removed his other obstacles which were yet in store for the party.

When the party had gone some distance further up the river, they came to two great boulders, one on each bank, which were clapping together across the stream. Bilantur first sang to these boulders, addressing them as *Batuh Bidi-up*, or "Clapping Stones". So sure was he of success, that as soon as he ended his song he thrust his paddle into the water and sent his boat surging forward to the gap between the boulders. The boulders clapped together. Bilantur leapt backwards and landed in the boat behind, as the swish of the water swamped his own. He was very badly shaken. "Really," he exclaimed, "this expedition is far too dangerous. I fear we shall all be slain by Minyawai. It's far too risky for us to go on."

After a little while he felt better. He appealed to other members of the party to try to stop the boulders clapping together, promising once more that he who succeeded should have Gumiloh as his wife. Again Silanting Kuning came forward and sang his song. The boulders stopped clapping. The party went past them on its way upstream.

Their troubles were still far from over. Before long great quantities of debris, such as leaves and sticks and branches, which usually sink to the bottom of the river, came floating down so thickly that soon the surface was completely covered over. Bilantur sang:

> 'O am Ahu gumuwab
> Nantih Ahu gumuwab
> . . . .'

> 'O, Rubbish, piling up!
> Pause, Rubbish, in your piling up.
> . . . .'

continuing as he had sung to the other obstacles. But the rubbish kept on pil ng up.

Silanting Kuning came forward. After again being promised Gumiloh's hand in marriage if he could make the rubbish sink, he sang to it his own song. The rubbish sank to the bottom. So the party went on.

Before long they rounded a bend to find that the river for the whole of the long reach up to the next bend was completely blocked with human bones. This was a barrier which really had been put in their way by Minyawai. The bones were the bones of men he had slain.

Bilantur was very frightened. "Look!" he exclaimed. "Look, all of you! See how many thousands Minyawai has killed. He will kill us, I know, and cast our bodies on to his heap!"

Patu spoke up. He would cut a channel through the bones. His knife had great power, he said. He sang to it:

'*O am Parang namang ku parisau!*
Dong daong parang lumpong!
Sabulan ku ngansah,
Sataun maseh tajam.
Lalat mbap pun mati,
Rambut nyampai sigih putus.
Tipau kiri tipau kanan,
Pampat bulat;
Ku mutoh abuh nkalilalu.'

'O, Knife, my great knife!
Dong, daong, my enormous knife!
Sharpened by me for a month,
To stay sharp for a year.
A fly settling there would be killed,
A hair falling there would be severed.
Slashing to the left, slashing to the right,
Cutting into pieces;
I will slay to the last man.'

He slashed at the bones. His knife bent.

Silanting Kuning came up. Bilantur and Patu both begged him to cut a channel through the bones. He sang to his knife—the knife called *Dong Daong Jamau Rampang*, which the Dragon-chief had given him:

'O am Dong Daong Jamau Rampang!
Sabulan ngansah,
Sataun maseh tajam.
Lalat mbap pun mati,
Rambut nyampai sigih putus.
Sintak isau bunyi kuning,
Bunyi uching diba ngaong,
Bunyi asuh diba knaong,
Bunyi babi bangkuwek,
Bunyi manok bangkukok,
Bunyi orang tua bikata,
Tisi dinding burung raya.[1]
Tipau kiri tipau kanan,
Pampat bulat,
Ku mutoh abuh nkalilalu,
Bala bala Minyawai Siludai Ali,
Nubah nungkal binua kami,
Nubah manok nyarang babi,
Mantang binua limon ari.'

'O, Dong Daong Jamau Rampang!
Sharpened for a month,
To stay sharp for a year.
A fly settling there would be killed,
A hair falling there would be halved.
It comes from its scabbard with great sound,
A sound like the caterwaul of a cat,
A sound like a dog howling,
A sound like a wild boar squealing,
A sound like a fowl crowing,
A sound like an old man talking.
. . . .
Slashing to the left, slashing to the right,
Cutting to pieces,
I will slay to the last man,
All the followers of Minyawai Siludai Ali,
Who raided our village,
Who stole our fowls, who killed our pigs,
Who destroyed our village in a time of peace.'

[1] These words literally mean 'at the wall, a very big bird'. Raseh said he did not know what their meaning, if any, was in the song, so we must leave them untranslated.

As he ended his song, he slashed at the bones. Rapidly he cleared a channel through them. So the canoes were soon able to pass on upstream.

The Dance of the Honey-tree

The party went on and on upstream for a long time without further trouble. At last they reached a spot where a very grand honey-tree was growing near the bank. This honey-tree was known as *tapang bintanun*, and it belonged to Gumiloh's father before Minyawai killed him. The party made camp beneath the tree. They first built a shelter. Then they cooked rice, and ate it. It was still not dark when they had finished their meal, so they decided to try to make the honey-tree dance.

Bilantur sang to the tree:

> '*O am Tapang Bintanun!*
> *Angkat nigal minari!*
> *Angkat manchah dibu langi!*'

> 'O, Bintanun Honey-tree!
> Get up and dance!
> Rise, clap, and spread your arms!'

The honey-tree did not stir.
Silanting Kuning then sang to the honey-tree:

> '*O am Tapang Bintanun!*
> *Angkat nigal minari!*
> *Angkat manchah dibu langi!*
> *Duloh ngadah pala*
> *Minyawai Siludai Ali.*'

> 'O, Bintanun Honey-tree!
> Get up and dance!
> Rise, clap, and spread your arms!
> To be the first to greet the head
> Of Minyawai Siludai Ali.'

The honey-tree began to dance. As its branches dipped low in one of the movements of the dance, Patu, in his pride, tried to chop one of them off. But his knife stuck in the wood, and the next moment was carried high into the sky, as the honey-tree swayed upwards again. The tree rested, with the knife far, far above the watchers below.

Patu, and then Bilantur, sang in an effort to make the honey-tree dance again, so that they might recover the knife. But the honey-tree would not move. Once more they appealed to Silanting Kuning for help. Silanting Kuning refused to give it. Patu and Bilantur had no choice but to climb the honey-tree by driving wooden spikes into its trunk up its whole lofty height. After long labour they came at last to the knife. But they could not pull it out. It was stuck as though it were joined to the branch in one single piece of iron. Patu wept.

When Silanting Kuning saw Patu weeping, he felt sorry for him. So he sang his song again, and again the honey-tree danced.

As the branch with the knife in it bent low, Patu grabbed the handle and tried to pull the knife out. It was stuck too fast, and the branch swung away with it. When the branch came down again, Silanting Kuning stretched up his foot and caught the handle of the knife between his toes. Easily, he drew the knife from the wood. Then, with his toes, he tossed it high up into the sky. When it came down again it struck a rock. The point pierced far into the rock, and stuck fast.

Patu tried to pull the knife from the rock. Laja tried. Kaleng tried. Sangau Labung tried. Bilantur tried. Nearly everybody tried. But it would not come away from the stone. Then Silanting Kuning grasped it, and easily drew it out. He gave it to Patu.

Patu tried to sharpen the knife. He worked at it for hours on a sharpening-stone, but it remained blunt. At last Silanting Kuning took hold of it. He bent it around the sharpening-stone so that the whole edge at once was pressed against the stone. He drew it quickly back and forth. In a twinkling it was extremely sharp.

It was now nearly sunset. The party prepared a hanging bamboo tray to hold offerings for the omen-birds of Minyawai,[1] and on it they placed small portions of cooked rice, eggs, tobacco, sections of dried nipah palm leaf in which to roll the tobacco for smoking, and pieces of areca-nut placed upon a green leaf together with a little lime

---

[1] The Land Dayaks take omens from particular actions of certain kinds of animals. Not all of these animals are in fact birds, although birds, by their flight or calls, provide the most frequent and many of the most important omens. However, the Dayaks apply the word *manuk*, or 'bird', generically to all omen-animals. For this reason we have translated it as 'omen-bird', even though the animals in question may prove to be deer or other species. In this case they turned out to be grasshoppers—a great joke at the enemy's expense, for how ridiculous to think of relying on grasshoppers for omens! After all the fanfares, too!

so as to be all ready for chewing. A short distance away they fixed in the ground a length of thick bamboo with its end splayed out to make a vase-like container. In it they placed eggs, cakes made of rice-flour and fat, powdered rice cooked in a different way,[1] pork, and cooked fowl. Then they called to the birds of Minyawai to come to the feast set out for them. Silanting Kuning sang:

'*King balai sinyih!*
Chong balai arang
Bintari Pasak Gandang!
Yu angkah yu Kiyau,
Yu api maan rantau,
Yu dumak Mamang,
Dengan Nyangau,
Yu ahab yu ranau!'[2]

'Come to the gathering in the headhouse!
Join the throng in the headhouse
Of Bintari Pasak Gandang!
Come with the cry of crows, come with the call of the Kiyau bird,
Come with the crackle of fire sweeping across a clearing,
Come with the roll of the drums of Mamang
And of Nyangau,
Come with a burst of shouting, come with a roar of cheering!'

Seven small grasshoppers appeared. They were the birds of Minyawai and of his six brothers. First they went to the hanging tray and took the offerings on it, then they ate those in the bamboo vase. When they had finished, each of them hopped into the coloured basket which Gumiloh had made for Silanting Kuning so that he could bring home Minyawai's head in it.

"Look!" cried out Pai Abang. "All the birds have gone into the stranger's basket. None of the rest of us will get heads. He will get them all."

After a moment, he spoke again, "Let us all try the eggs to test our courage. If from any man's egg a cock comes forth, that man is brave. If a hen comes forth, he is a coward."

When everybody had taken up an egg, Bilantur sang:

[1] Delicacies cooked for festivals. Portions of each variety of food eaten at festivals are always laid out in this way for the omen-birds.
[2] Mythological characters.

> '*Tateh raneh tatau randau*
> *Banturah batuh tamau*
> *Pechet ku taluh*
> *Jaji jagau!*'
>
> '. . . . .
> . . . .
> When I break this egg
> A cock it will become!'

He cracked his egg. A hen came out. All the other men cracked their eggs. Hens came out.

Pai Abang said, "Clearly we will get no heads. First all the birds went into this stranger's coloured basket, and now hens have come from all our eggs. If any of us get any heads at all, they can only be those of fools, or of the blind, or of the sick. We cannot get the heads of the leaders. None of us can hope to get the head of Minyawai."

Silanting Kuning took up an egg. He sang:

> '*Tateh raneh tatau randau*
> *Banturah batuh tamau*
> *Pechet ku taluh*
> *Jaji jagau,*
> *Bada ku yu kandang*
> *Tadah rantau.*'
>
> '. . . . .
> . . . .
> When I crack this egg
> A cock it will become,
> Which I'll make to call as a magpie
> Out in a clearing.'

He cracked his egg. A cock sprang forth, and crowed lustily in the midst of the party.

"Ah!" exclaimed Pai Abang. "See! It is a cock! The stranger has got a cock from his egg. He will recover the head of Gumiloh's father from Minyawai. And he will slay Minyawai himself."

Silanting Kuning Reveals his Secret Name

Night came on. When it was dark, they set out one after another to look for the enemy. Bilantur went first. After a while he came to a place where the track was very narrow with a great precipice on each side. Lying right across the track was an enormous vine. He returned to tell the others that the way was blocked.

In the morning he led the rest of the party to the place to clear away the vine to let them pass along. Before the work began, Bilantur sang to his knife, ending his song:

> *'Tipau kiri tipau kanan,*
> *Pampat bulat,*
> *Ku bungkung kayu Bayut!'*

> 'Slashing to the left, slashing to the right,
> Chopping into bits,
> I'll cut away this *Bayut* vine!'

As he finished singing, he smote mightily at the vine. His knife buckled. The vine was unbruised.

Bilantur asked his followers to try. He asked Laja. He asked Kaleng. He asked Sangau Labung. He asked everybody. But all refused, because they had seen what had happened to Bilantur's knife, and they feared for their own. When no one else would try, Bilantur asked Silanting Kuning.

Silanting Kuning sang to his knife the song he had sung to it before, but ending:

> *'Tipau kiri tipau kanan,*
> *Pampat bulat,*
> *Ku bungkung kayu Bayut!'*

> 'Slashing to the left, slashing to the right,
> Chopping into bits,
> I'll cut away this *Bayut* vine!'

He slashed at the vine. At his first stroke, it flew apart and tumbled away, one half down each precipice. Where the vine had been there was now a deep hole in the middle of the track. Silanting Kuning looked down the hole. Far below he saw the roof of the house of Singiyang Naga the Dragon-chief.

"Come here, all of you!" he cried to the others. "Come and see my grandfather's house!"

Everybody came up to peer down the hole. When they had all seen the house, Silanting Kuning told them, "I must go down there to spend a night with my grandfather. The rest of you carry on with your scouting." Then he climbed down the hole.

That evening Bilantur set out once more to scout. He had gone only a mile or two when he came to a bridge. It was a single log placed over a shallow stream-bed. Just as he was about to step on the bridge, the bridge said, "Don't dare come to make war on our village! Go home, or else you will all die in our village." Bilantur went back to his camp.

He told Kaleng to go out scouting instead of him. Kaleng refused. He told Patu. Patu refused. He told the others, one after another, but they all refused, because they were very frightened. Last of all, he told Pai Abang. Pai Abang said he would go.

Pai Abang went forward boldly until he met the bridge. The bridge spoke. It spoke to him as it had spoken to Bilantur. Pai Abang received a great shock. He hurried back to camp very frightened.

Later in the night Silanting Kuning returned from the house of the Dragon-chief. Straight away he set out to do the scouting himself. He came to the bridge. As he was about to step on it, the bridge exclaimed, "Don't dare come to make war on our village! Go back home, or else you will all die in our village."

"That's what you think," replied Silanting Kuning, "but I shan't be left dead in Minyawai's village. Instead I will slay Minyawai, and dry his head." Thereupon he kicked the bridge. The bridge broke in two, and began to cry.

Silanting Kuning went on his way. Soon he came to some wooden effigies guarding the approach to Minyawai's longhouses,[1] of which there were three in his village. The biggest effigy said, "Don't dare make war against our village! If you do, you will leave your body here."

"No, I won't leave my body in your village," answered Silanting Kuning. "I will kill Minyawai, and dry his head in my kitchen." Thereupon he kicked all the effigies away. They wept. Silanting Kuning strode on past them.

In a few moments he came to the village bathing-place. There he met Antu Ayih, or the Water-demon, and this demon's wife. They threatened him as the effigies had done. After giving them the same

[1] During large festivals, roughly carved effigies are often placed beside the tracks leading into the village to warn away demons, and are left there until they rot, their rotting sometimes serving as a reminder that the time has come for another large festival.

answer, he grabbed hold of them, and broke their arms and legs. Then he tossed away the husband upstream, and tossed away the wife downstream. Both cried.

He went up the steps from the bathing-place. The steps threatened him. He kicked them to pieces. They wept.

He went on towards the longhouses. Quite close to them he came upon a bush of *chinchung dayah* flowers and a bush of *bunga kamang* flowers. The bushes warned him to come no further. He plucked a flower from each to stick them behind his ears. Then he leapt from the ground right up on to the verandah of the longhouse, without even touching the steps.

On the verandah he met a firefly. He said to the firefly, "Be kind enough to lead me to the room of the girl whom Minyawai wishes to marry."

The firefly led him straight to the girl's bed. He went inside her mosquito-net. When he came very close to her, she woke up, exclaiming, "Where is our head?" She was thinking of the head of Gumiloh's father. She wanted to be quite sure that nothing had happened to it. She asked about it because she thought her visitor was Minyawai.

Silanting Kuning was very clever. "There it is!" he answered, "in the coloured basket over there on the wall." Then he went on, "But we must be on guard. Tomorrow everyone must stay in the village, for Kichapi intends to fight us."

Silanting Kuning said this because it was already known in the village that Minyawai had had a dream in which he had been told by the Dragon-chief that an enemy called Kichapi was going to fight against him. He himself was really that enemy. Kichapi was a secret name which had been given to him by the Seven-headed Giant. He wanted the enemy to know who he really was when he came. He also wished to deceive the girl into thinking that it was Minyawai speaking. These were the reasons why he spoke his secret name now.

He lay down beside the girl, and made love to her for the rest of the night. Just before dawn, he went to the headhouse. There he broke into pieces the spear, the fighting-knife and the shield of Minyawai, and made a hole in his drum. He next searched until he found the heads of the mother and father of Gumiloh. He took them back with him to his camp, which was downstream a little way from the camp of Bilantur. Then he went to sleep. When day came, he went on sleeping. The uncles of Gumiloh began to cook food.

Minyawai Issues a Challenge

In the morning in Minyawai's village the girl awoke, and sought Minyawai. She found him still asleep. "Oh, why," she shouted, "did Minyawai tell me that Kichapi was coming to make war against our village today, and yet sleeps late in the morning?"

"No!" cried Minyawai, jumping up. "I did not tell you that! I did not visit you last night! It must have been Kichapi himself! I had no plan to make war against him today. It must be his plan to make war against me."

He rushed off to the headhouse to get his fighting-knife. He found it broken to pieces. So he took the knife of the girl's father. Then he gathered together his six brothers and the girls they were betrothed to, and his own betrothed. This made fourteen in his party altogether. They set off downstream to attack Silanting Kuning—or rather, Kichapi, since this was the name by which he was known to them. To his own party he was known just as the stranger.

Minyawai and his followers went straight past Bilantur's camp. Bilantur and his men threw spears at them. They took no notice. They went on downstream towards the camp of Kichapi. When they drew near, they got out of their canoes, and walked quietly up to the camp.

Kichapi was still asleep. The uncles were still cooking food. Minyawai and his followers came very close to Kichapi, and sat around him in a circle. Gumiloh's uncles were too frightened to speak. They just went on cooking food, as though nothing had happened. Then the seven men and the seven girls, sitting in a ring around Kichapi, sang:

> 'O am Samih, tidu ngalantu,
> Minyak rida rida.
> Hari siang pigangang!'

> 'O Friend, in very deep sleep,
> Slumbering so heavily.
> The day is far advanced!'

Kichapi awoke. He stood up. The party sitting around him did not make a move against him. He stepped through them and walked down to the bathing-place, where he washed himself with soap made from vegetable oil. He returned to his shelter, in the centre of the ring of enemies. He sat down to comb his hair.

When Kichapi had finished combing his hair, Minyawai, without speaking a word, prepared a piece of areca-nut for chewing, and offered it to him on the end of his spear. This was a challenge. Kichapi took the areca-nut off the spear, put it in his mouth, and began to chew it. This meant he had accepted the challenge. Kichapi himself then prepared areca-nut, and offered it to Minyawai on the end of his own spear. Minyawai took it off the spear, and began to chew it.

The food which Gumiloh's uncles had been cooking was now ready. They took it off the fire, and shared it out amongst everybody present. The girls who were betrothed to the six brothers of Minyawai each ate with the brother to whom she was betrothed. But the betrothed of Minyawai did not wish to eat with him. She went to eat with Kichapi instead.

Silanting Kuning, Known Now as Kichapi, Fights Minyawai

When they had all finished eating, Minyawai said to Kichapi, "Why did you sleep with my Love last night? For a long time have I been betrothed to her, and yet I have never slept with her."

Kichapi sang in answer:

'*Rindu ku tidu dengan dih dayung bagus gilah,*
Tubuh nya basai tujuh satah,
Rambut nya panyai siribu dapah.'

'I wished to sleep with a maid of shining beauty,
Her body seven forearms long,[1]
Her hair a thousand arm-spreads long.'

Minyawai then sang to Kichapi,

'*O am Samih!*
Apa dama urih
Nuan nchamih?'

'O, my Friend!
What is the name of the medicine
Belonging to you, my Friend?'

---

[1] One of the qualities in the Dayak ideal of feminine beauty is height.

Kichapi sang in answer,

'Ada mah urih aku nchamih!
Urih kirubung kura mah urih aku;
Bukoh rabang raput mah urih aku;
Pichung kirubit babah mah urih aku;
Kura rinda rijabung jawa kura panchir pingawa;
Berih akih ku Singiyang Naga,
Berih adi ku dayang Silujah,
Betutup sanang Jawa,
Bidingding Tajau Lingka.
Chilah chilar singkap pingan
Pijinak mata tidur;
Bikata burung raya
Berih akih ku Antu Muta pirapa raya.
Pakaking siruh bauh; bigangang uhat kayuh;
Bubut babi; pimungkam bubut buhang;
Mah urih aku.'

'There is medicine possessed by me, my Friend!
Medicine made from tortoise-shell, that is my medicine;
A fighting-knife with a chip in the blade, that is my medicine;
A bottle with a broken top, that is my medicine;
A shell of the *rinda* tortoise with its tuft of hair, and a shell of the
          panchir pingawa tortoise;
Which were given to me by Singiyang Naga,
Given to me by his younger sister, the maiden Silujah,[1]
Who are wealthy in Javanese gongs,
Rich in the jars called *Tajau Lingka*.
Glittering pieces of plate
To drowse the eyes;
Feathers of the huge bird
Which were given to me by the Seven-headed Giant of the
          great swamp.
The claws of an eagle; an up-grown root of a tree;
The tusks of a wild boar; a charm of bear's teeth;
This is the medicine belonging to me.'

[1] Earlier the maiden was described as the granddaughter of the Dragon-chief. This
was probably a slip which reflects the strong bond of affection generally existing today
between Dayak grandfathers and their granddaughters, whereas the story itself may have
originated in a different cultural setting with which the words of the song, being less open
to variation, continue to accord.

Minyawai was angered at hearing this long list of medicines. "You have very many things as your medicines," he exclaimed, "far too many indeed!"

Kichapi replied, "All right, then. Tell me what your own medicine is."

Minyawai sang:

'*Ada mah urih aku.*
Kiribung kura mah urih aku;
Bukoh rabang raput mah urih aku;
Pimungkam bubut babi;
Pimangah bubut buhang;
Mah urih aku!'

'There is medicine belonging to me.
The shell of a tortoise, that is my medicine;
A fighting-knife with a chip in the blade, that is my medicine;
A charm of tusks of a wild boar;
A charm of the teeth of a bear;
That is the medicine belonging to me.'

Minyawai then asked Kichapi, "What is your spear like?"

Kichapi sang in answer:

'*Anang tanyah tanyah lunyu aku!*
Tuh pangalunyuh dayung balu!
Nadai kala labuh tanah!
Labuh ningang tangkai ati!'

'Don't dare mention my spear!
It makes widows!
It never strikes the ground!
It always strikes the hearts of men!'

Minyawai was very frightened on hearing this. He knew that the spear he had could not compare, because it was his father-in-law's spear, and not his own. Therefore he decided to change his choice of weapons from spears to blowpipes with poisoned arrows. Kichapi agreed to the change.

Minyawai slipped a poisoned arrow into his blowpipe and shot it straight at Kichapi's eye. It hit his eye, but it did not penetrate. It just bounced off.

Kichapi had got an arrow into his blowpipe. He shot it at an eye of Minyawai. The arrow missed his eye. It just grazed Minyawai's forehead, stinging it with the poison.

Minyawai then threw his spear at Kichapi, yelling, "Hold up your shield to try to protect yourself!" But his aim was bad. The spear passed between Kichapi's legs, doing no more harm than to rip his loin-cloth.

"Ah, now is my turn!" cried Kichapi. "Line up, you seven brothers! One behind the other, with Minyawai in front! And none of you step out of line!"

He hurled his spear. It passed right through Minyawai, and right through the next five of his brothers. As it struck each brother he called out to those behind him to jump out of the way. Only the last in the line, the youngest brother of Minyawai, had time to jump away. He escaped. His name was Kirudu Kuru Batu. Minyawai and all his other brothers were killed.

Kichapi cut off the heads of Minyawai and his five slain brothers, and gave the heads to the uncles of Gumiloh for them to put in the camp. He let the uncles do the skinning of the heads.

Kichapi Pursues the Last of Minyawai's Brothers

Kichapi also told the uncles to bring from his camp all of his medicine, as he was going to fight Kirudu Kuru Batu, the youngest brother of Minyawai. When they brought it to him, he tied it all to his waist. Then he attacked Kirudu.

All day long the two of them fought, moving back and forth, slashing at each other with their knives, but neither succeeded in wounding the other. Their knives would not cut the flesh.

At last, as the day was drawing to a close, Kirudu dropped his knife, and seized Kichapi in his arms. He lifted him up and dashed him against a tree. Kichapi was unhurt. In return, he seized Kirudu, and dashed him against a tree. Kirudu was unhurt. Kichapi lifted him up again, and dashed him to the ground. Kirudu was still unhurt. He jumped to his feet, and, seizing Kichapi, slammed him so hard to the ground that Kichapi sank up to his knees in it. He was unhurt. He picked up Kirudu, and slammed him up to his waist in the ground. Kirudu was unhurt. He slammed Kichapi into the ground up to his waist. Kichapi was unhurt. He picked up Kirudu, and sent him smack into the ground right up to his neck. Kirudu was unhurt. He rose up. He seized Kichapi. He slammed him down harder than ever. This time he slammed him down so hard that he broke right through the crust of the earth. He fell on downwards, and landed right on the roof of the house of Singiyang Naga the Dragon-chief. He decided to spend the night with the Dragon-chief.

On the surface of the earth, after Kichapi had disappeared through it, Kirudu Kuru Batu called together all the animals of the countryside and jungle. He prepared a feast for them. He told them that he was going to fly away into the sky, and that he wanted them all to keep it a secret from Kichapi as to where he had gone. He then invited them all to eat their fill at his feast. But there was one little animal which would not eat any of the feast. This animal was a flying lemur, called Pigo Bang Pigong.

When the feast was over, Kirudu flew up into the sky. In the sky, he met Tayung Kilimayuh, the old woman who had boiled up Silanting Kuning to make him handsome. She knew what had been going on down below on the earth. She knew that Kirudu must hide. So she pointed out a coconut palm, of the yellow kind, and told him to climb up to sleep inside one of the coconuts. Kirudu could do this because he was able to make himself big or small at will. He went to sleep inside a coconut.

In the morning Kichapi returned to the surface of the earth from the home of his grandfather, the Dragon-chief. He asked the first animal he met where Kirudu was. The animal said it did not know. He asked another animal, and got the same reply. He asked animal after animal, until there was only one left, but all said they did not know. The last animal was the flying lemur, Pigo Bang Pigong. He said to Pigo Bang Pigong, "Tell me, please, where Kirudu is." "He has already flown away up into the sky," answered Pigo Bang Pigong.

Kichapi immediately flew up to the sky himself. He went straight to the house of Grandmother Kilimayuh. "Grandmother," he said, "I am very thirsty. I should like to climb that coconut palm to get a coconut to drink."

"Oh, don't climb that one!" she exclaimed, "not that one of the yellow kind! That kind of coconut is not so nice. Climb one of the ordinary kind of palms, where the coconuts are bigger."

She was, of course, trying to protect Kirudu who was hiding in one of the nuts on the yellow palm. But Kichapi knew that he was there. So he replied, "No! I think that coconuts of the yellow kind are much nicer." And up the palm he went.

He pulled off one coconut, sliced off the top of the shell, and drank the milk inside. Then he pulled off a second one. But just as he was about to slice off the top, a voice from within cried, "Don't cut! I'm inside!" and out jumped Kirudu. Once out of the coconut he was back to his usual size. He climbed down to the ground with Kichapi.

The two of them then flew down to the earth together, and set out along the track to Minyawai's village. On their way they passed Bilantur's camp. Kichapi called out to Bilantur, "Now is the time! Lead your men to the attack on the village of Minyawai!" He then walked on with Kirudu until they reached the village. They went straight up into the headhouse.

As soon as they were inside the headhouse, Kirudu threw himself upon Kichapi's mercy. "Don't kill me!" he begged. "I will do anything for you! I'll be your servant! I'll carry away your excrement!"

"I will not spare you," said Kichapi. "I am going to kill you."

Kirudu saw that there was no hope for him. Thereupon he called for the girls who had been betrothed to his six slain brothers and the girl to whom he himself was betrothed. When the girls had gathered in the headhouse, he addressed them, saying: "I am about to die. Nothing can stop that. But one thing I want to say to you first. It is this. When I am dead, none of you must go with this man back to his village to take part in the festival for my head. For if you do take part in that festival, great harm will befall you."

Having spoken, Kirudu stretched out one of his legs towards Kichapi. Kichapi held up his fighting-knife, and sang to it, ending his song:

> '*Tipau kiri tipau kanan,*
> *Pampat bulat!*
> *Ku mutoh abuh bala Minyawai,*
> *Dengan Kirudu Kuru Batu,*
> *Tijuh biradih.*'

> 'Slashing to the left, slashing to the right,
> Cutting into bits!
> I slay the whole family of Minyawai,
> And now Kirudu Kuru Batu,
> The seventh of the brothers.'

Down came his knife and off went Kirudu's leg. Then Kichapi cut off his other leg. Then he cut off each of his arms. Finally he cut off his head.

Kirudu's body was left to rot in the headhouse, because there was no one left alive in the village to look after it. All the people had been slain in the meantime by Bilantur's party.

Bilantur himself managed to kill only one man. He was a man with ringworm all through the roots of his hair. So all he got was one worm-ridden head. He was very pleased, but it did not seem quite enough. So he cut off a dog's head as well. Then he hurried in triumph right back to Gumiloh's village. He wanted to be the first conqueror to return. He took the heads straight to Gumiloh. One look at them was enough for her. "This is not the head of Minyawai!" she exclaimed. "It's a dog's head! And this other one is the head of a pitiful, diseased man!" So saying, she threw the heads away in disgust.

Bilantur was filled with shame. He would not stay in Gumiloh's house. He went back to his own boat at the landing-place.

The remainder of Bilantur's party, together with Kichapi, did not follow the bad example of Bilantur in rushing straight back home. When they left the village of Minyawai, they returned to their camp. Then they sent two men, Bunga Kambang and Chinchung Dayah, to Gumiloh's village to let the people know that the war-party was about to return.

When the two men arrived with this news, Gumiloh asked, "Who has got Minyawai's head?"

"The stranger has it," they answered. "And he is also bringing back the heads of your mother and father."

Kichapi was, of course, still known only as the stranger to the people of Gumiloh's village. Silanting Kuning was the name given to him by his parents, and Kichapi that given to him by the Seven-headed Giant, but the people knew neither of these names. To them he had been known first as an orang-utan and then simply as a mysterious man from whence nobody knew.

The Victors Return

Gumiloh began preparations for the return of the conquerors. She spread out mats, and told the people to gather for the festival. The main ceremonies were to be held on the part of the longhouse verandah outside her house.

The warriors came. First came those led by Patu, then those led by Laja, then those led by Sangau Labung, then those led by Kaleng, and then all the rest. Pai Abang and Kichapi were last, a good way behind. When they arrived close to the landing-place, the others waited until Pai Abang and Kichapi came up.

Kichapi had brought with him the heads of Minyawai and all his six brothers. He also brought with him the seven girls to whom they had been betrothed. But five of the girls he had changed into eggs. The other two, who were very pretty, he had sitting one on each side of him in his canoe.

The whole war-party moved up to the landing-place. All the young girls and women waded out to meet them. Gumiloh stepped over the other boats making straight for Kichapi's boat. When she reached it, she pushed the two women head over heels into the water, exclaiming, "What right have you to bring the wives of our enemies here?"

"What right have you to push *my* two wives into the water?" retorted Kichapi.

The two girls recovered from their ducking, and reached the landing-place. Kichapi then led them up to the verandah of the long-house, where the festival had already begun. The gongs were sounding, some people were dancing, and the priests and priestesses were making the first offerings to the ancestors and the demons. Gumiloh followed Kichapi, carrying the heads of Minyawai and his six brothers, and the heads of her mother and father. The seven new heads were still not dry.

On the verandah, Pai Abang's wife was wearing a ripe banana in her hair in place of a comb.

Everyone sat down on the verandah. Then women began to dance with the heads, to greet them. Gumiloh danced to greet the head of Minyawai. She did not, of course, dance with the heads of her mother and father, because this must not be done.

When the heads of the enemies had been danced with for a little while, they were laid on the inner verandah. The people all went to bathe in the river. On their return to their houses, they dressed in their best clothes. Then they gathered again on the inner verandah to eat together. There was plenty of the nicest foods—*pulit* rice cooked in bamboo, pork, fowl, preserved fish, and all the special festival delicacies.

When the eating had slowed down, one of Gumiloh's uncles, Buku Tabu, began to beat a drum, and the other uncle, Tungu Linau, began to beat small gongs. As they did so, Kichapi sang:

> *'O am Buku Tabu biduan Tungu Linau!*
> *Tubah kan gundang!*

Aku nyuruh dih dayang dara Gumiloh
Angkat nigal minari,
Angkat manchah kibu langi,
Ngadah pala Minyawai Siludai Ali!'

'O, Buku Tabu and Tungu Linau!
Sound the drum, beat the gongs!
I wish to have the dear maiden Gumiloh
Rise to dance,
Rise, clap, and spread her arms,
To greet the head of Minyawai Siludai Ali!'

Gumiloh rose to dance. She danced holding a head in each hand.
When she had danced with them for a while, she stopped to exchange
them for another two. Then she danced again. She danced until she
had danced with all the heads of Minyawai and his six brothers.

But she danced without a cloth. She should have had a cloth draped
over her shoulders, with an end held in each hand. Kichapi called out
to her to get a cloth. But Gumiloh had none, she had never danced
with heads before, so she had not felt the need of one. When Kichapi
saw that she was at a loss, he sang:

'Dini pirachah inah Mayang Piduka,
Sinyipat bunyi kilat,
Ginaur bunyi guntur,
Pingampuh pulau bubung pati?'

'Where is your dancing-cloth called *Mayang Piduka*,
Flowing with lightning flash,
Making a roar like thunder,
Booming through jungle and hills and loftiest peaks?'

As he ended his song, he snatched a cloth from the shoulders of
one of the two girls from Minyawai's village. As he swept it through
the air it became a dazzling sheet of lightning; he waved it and
thunder surged in a mighty roar.

So sudden and loud was the thunder that Bilantur, sleeping in his
boat at the landing-stage, awoke with such a start that he capsized
into the river. This put him in a terrible rage. As soon as he could
recover his voice, he yelled out to all the people in the village, "Just
you wait! I will lead all my followers here to wipe you out!"

Kichapi handed the cloth to Gumiloh. She took it, and began to dance once again with the heads. As she danced, Kichapi sang to her:

> '*Riga riga tubu,*
> *Dih nanda rupa bintang tumuh di langit,*
> *Liga ligai rupa padi tanam tatai,*
> *Liga liguh rupa padi tanam munguh*
>
> . . . .
>
> *Tunguh badunchul rupa bungkung kaya baka kaul!*'

> 'Your body moves in rhythm,
> Glinting like the stars in the sky,[1]
> Waving like the paddy by the longhouse,
> Rippling like the paddy on the sunny hill-sides
>
> . . . .
>
> Your stomach bulges like a vine, now thick, now thin!'

The last line Kichapi did not intend to apply to Gumiloh. He had been singing to her, but he could not help taking notice of Pai Abang's wife, who was also dancing, although she was large with a child. She did not look at all graceful, and Kichapi meant the last line for her. But Gumiloh thought it was meant for herself, and felt so ashamed that she stopped dancing.

Kichapi thereupon got up to dance with the heads. Pai Abang joined him. As they danced, Gumiloh sang to Kichapi:

> '*Riga riga tubu,*
> *Muh nanda rupa bulan . . .*'

> 'Your body moves in rhythm,
> Gleaming like the moon . . .'

The rest of her song was the same as that of Kichapi. But she, too, did not mean the last line for Kichapi. She meant it for Pai Abang. Kichapi realized this, and took no offence.

The dancing went on for the rest of the night, sometimes with the heads and sometimes not. When dawn came the people rested.

---

[1] A reference to her silver belt.

Bilantur Declares War

In the morning, after the dancing had stopped, Kichapi went down to the landing-place. He remembered Bilantur's threat of the night before. He wished to know whether he still kept to it. Bilantur was in his boat. Kichapi went up to him, and said, "Do you really intend to bring your people here to fight us?"

"Yes," answered Bilantur, "I am coming back with a war-party to slay you all."

This reply made Kichapi wild. He seized Bilantur, and cut off one of his ears and the tip of his nose. Then he pushed him backwards, exclaiming, "Go and fetch your war-party!"

Bilantur set off downstream for his village. When at last he came in sight of it, all the small boys of the village gathered at the landing-place to see him arrive. As he came closer to them they began to yell, "Here comes Bilantur, wearing red flowers in his ear and on his nose!"

Bilantur swore at the children, and chased them away, calling out as he did so, "If I hadn't been wounded like this, all of Minyawai's men would have been slain by me!"

He went up to his house. His mother and father dressed his wounds with leaves of the kind to make them heal.

When the wounds were healed Bilantur called a village meeting. Its purpose was to arrange an expedition against Kichapi and Gumiloh's village. The people were all in favour of his scheme.

The expedition was prepared, and in due course the war-party set off. But all their boats were made of brass. Whenever they brushed a log in the river, they clanged. As they neared Gumiloh's village, the children heard them coming. Some ran to Gumiloh to tell her. The rest hastened to tell other people.

Pai Abang hurried to Gumiloh, and asked, "Where is your friend?"

"He is asleep," she replied.

"Well, wake him up quickly! Bilantur is coming!"

Gumiloh did so at once. She was very excited. She told him Bilantur was almost upon them. He must rise quickly.

"Don't worry," said Kichapi, stretching. "It's quite all right. Bilantur often comes here to make trade, to sell us salt, and so on. He's quite welcome to come."

He then got up, taking his time. He strolled down to the landing-place, quite unarmed. Almost as soon as he reached it, Bilantur's party arrived.

Leading the party was a huge giant. His name was Atong Pala Tiga, or the Three-headed Giant. Kichapi sang to him.

> 'O am Atong Pala Tiga!
> Balit smua kita balit!
> Amat kita beribu laksa,
> Ndah teriken jarum China,
> Sakulak langah mampah,
> Ndah teriken antu duah,
> Ndah sukup kita lawan aku!
> Balit kita smua balit!'

> 'O Three-headed Giant!
> Turn back all you, away with you!
> Although you be a thousand strong,
> As countless as Chinese needles are,
> As a coconut-shellful of sunflower seeds,
> More than a couple of demons could manage to count.
> You lack the strength to withstand me!
> Turn back all you, away with you!'

The Three-headed Giant sang in answer:

> 'O am Samih!
> Ndah mah kameh balit.
> Mati kameh untung sibayan;
> Idup kameh untung manang bilian.'

> 'My Friend!
> We won't turn back.
> If we should die, the after-world will gain;
> If we should live, the manang then will gain.'

He meant by this last line that if they were victorious a great feast of celebration would be held under the direction of the spirit-medium. It would be different from the festival which was held in Gumiloh's village, because Bilantur's people were Malays.

Kichapi then said to Bilantur, "Give me your fighting-knife."

Bilantur handed it to him. He did so because his heart was already weakened by the power of Kichapi's medicine.

Kichapi held up the knife. He sang to it the song he usually sang to his own knife, ending:

'*Mutoh abuh nkali lalu*
Bala Atong Pala Tiga!'

'I shall slay to the very last man,
All the troop of the Three-headed Giant!'

As he ended his song, he strode forward into the middle of the war-party. He fought with man after man until he had cut off all their heads except those of the Three-headed Giant and Bilantur. These two alone were still unhurt. Kichapi paused. He sang to the uncles of Gumiloh:

'*O am Buku Tabu biduan Tungu Linau!*
Bawa situh uri ku,
Sudi mandi ntama bisa jaya,
Ngau ku ngilawan Atong Pala Tiga,
Berih akih ku Singiyang Naga.'

'O Buku Tabu and Tungu Linau!
Bring here my medicine,
So powerful, potent, active, strong,
For me to fight this Three-headed Giant,
A gift to me from Singiyang Naga.'

Then he sang on about his medicine as he had sung about it before he slew Minyawai.

The uncles of Gumiloh brought him the medicine. As he took it from them, he sang:

'*O am Samih!*
Mati nuan ilah mati!
Balu bini nuan ilah balu!'

'O my Friends!
You'll die, you'll die quite soon!
And widows, widows soon your wives will be!'

The Three-headed Giant sang in reply:

'*Badau mah aku toh mati!*
Pala ku maseh agang!
Tubuh ku maseh ringang ringang!'

'Not yet have I been slain!
These heads of mine remain erect!
This trunk of mine stands upright still!'

Kichapi had thrown aside Bilantur's fighting-knife. His own had now been brought to him. He raised it up and sang to it the song he always sang to it when he had special work for it to do. Then he was ready to launch his attack. But the Three-headed Giant was very tall. He was as tall as a honey-tree. His heads were far above Kichapi. So Kichapi leapt. He took a mighty leap. He leapt right up to the height of the giant, and cut off one of his heads.

"There you are!" he cried, as the head came tumbling down. "You'll soon die! Your wife will soon be a widow!"

"Ah, no!" said the Three-headed Giant. "I'll not die yet! I still have two heads!"

Kichapi sprang again, and sliced off a second head.

"There you are!" he cried. "Now you'll soon be dead! Soon your wife will be a widow!"

"No!" said the Three-headed Giant. "I'll not die yet. I still have one head left!"

A third time Kichapi leapt. He cut off the last head of the Three-headed Giant. The giant's body tottered. Then it came crashing to earth with a roar louder than that of a great forest tree falling.

Kichapi turned to Bilantur. He grabbed him in one hand. With the other he cut off his remaining ear and took another slice off his nose. Then he pushed him backwards, saying, "Go! And if you wish, fetch another war-party! And be sure you make it a lot stronger than this one!"

Bilantur hastened away in his canoe as fast as he could. Again, when he drew near to the landing-place at his village, the children gathered there cried out, "Here comes Bilantur wearing red flowers on his ear and on his nose!"

Bilantur raged at them, shouting out, "If I had not been wounded like this, I should have slain all Kichapi's band!"

His mother and father once more treated his nose and his ear until they were healed. Then Bilantur called another meeting to arrange a second expedition against Kichapi.

Bilantur Tries Again

The new expedition was placed under the command of Atong Pala Tujuh, a giant with seven heads.

The Seven-headed Giant saw that the warriors left in Bilantur's village were too few to make a strong war-party. So many had been killed in the last attack on Kichapi. Therefore he sent messengers to the Dayak village where Silanting Kuning, who was now Kichapi, had been born. He told the messengers that they were to seek the help of this village against Kichapi. Of course, no one in the village knew that the famous and feared Kichapi was really the same person as the little boy from their village who had disappeared only a few days after his birth. They saw no reason why they should not help Bilantur's village, with which they were friendly, against the enemy who had caused it so much trouble. Many men went back with the messengers to join the war-party of the Seven-headed Giant. Amongst them were all the six brothers of Kichapi. Their names were Mamang Marak, Mamang Marau, Mamang Tangah, Mamang Malabau, Mamang Kalimunut, and Lintang Tabang.

The war-party was now very strong. It numbered about two thousand men.

The war-party set off upstream. As it neared Gumiloh's village, the clanging of the brass boats again gave warning of its coming. The children ran to Pai Abang to tell him that the war-party was drawing close. Pai Abang rushed to Gumiloh. Gumiloh woke Kichapi. Kichapi yawned, and said, "Don't fuss. It's quite all right. Let Bilantur come. He often comes here to trade, to sell us salt fish, and so on."

The children came running up again. "Bilantur's party is very big!" they cried, "and they have with them a giant with seven heads!"

Kichapi got up from his bed. He went up into the headhouse. From this height, he could see Bilantur's army.

He left the headhouse to walk down to the landing-place. There he met the enemy army. He told them to go home again. He sang to them as he had done to the first war-party. His song was the same, except that it was addressed to the Seven-headed Giant instead of to the Three-headed Giant.

The Seven-headed Giant answered just as his predecessor had done.

Kichapi went back to his house to get his fighting-knife. He walked down towards the landing-place again. When he was half way to it, he suddenly leapt at a tree. He leapt high into the air. As he flew up, he sliced the tree in half. As the part with the branches on it fell down, he settled on top of the stump, thirty feet above the ground.

Sitting on his lofty perch, he called down to Gumiloh and her sister Kumang Malidi to spread mats at the landing-place and to set out areca-nut with leaves and lime ready for chewing.

Gumiloh and her sister did as they were asked. They then sat on the mats together with the seven girls who had been betrothed to Minyawai and his six brothers.

Then Kichapi sang to the uncles of Gumiloh to fetch his medicine. He sang as he had sung to them before, but this time he ended his song:

'Ntama ku bisa,
Berih akih ku Antu Mutah,
Mulah nama;
Akih ku Antu Bilitu,
Mulah nama aku;
Akih ku Antu Rigasih,
Mulah nama ku,
Kichapi pimungkam!
Barah api,
Pimadam mata ari!'

'My potent medicine,
Given to me by the Seven-headed Giant,
He who bestowed my name;
Given to me by the giant Bilitu,
Who gave a name to me;
Given to me by the giant Rigasih,
He who bestowed this name of mine,
The name of Kichapi!
Which glows like fire
And can eclipse the sun!'[1]

Then he shouted, "Mamang Marak, Mamang Marau, Mamang Tangah, Mamang Malabau, Mamang Kalimunut, Lintang Tabang are my brothers!"

[1] This refers to the medicine, not to the name. The word *pimadam* means 'to make ill'. It is not that the brilliance of the medicine will outshine the sun, but that the medicine has the power to make the sun sicken, this being believed to be the cause of an eclipse. It will be remembered that Silanting Kuning earlier used the medicine to produce this effect first to allow him to take a bath unseen and, on the second occasion, to visit Gumiloh.

"Ah!" the brothers exclaimed. "This must be our youngest brother!"

They immediately left Bilantur's party to hurry towards Kichapi. But Kichapi called out, "Don't come over here to me. Sit on the mats with your sisters-in-law."

The brothers sat on the mats with Gumiloh, Kumang Malidi and the other girls. When the rest of the men from the village of Kichapi's birth saw his brothers change sides, they too all went over, because they had no wish to fight their friends.

Kichapi jumped down from the tree. He walked up to the enemy. He lifted up his fighting-knife. He sang to it as he always sang to it at such times, except that he ended:

'*Pampat bulat mutoh abuh*
Bala Atong Pala Tujuh!'

'Cutting into pieces, slaying everyone
All the party of the Seven-headed Giant!'

He then sang to Gumiloh:

'*O am dih dayung dara Gumiloh!*
Bawa baju bulu pake terbang,
Ngau ngilawan Atong Pala Tujuh!'

'O my dearest lady Gumiloh!
Bring here my coat of feathers with power to fly,
For me to battle with the Seven-headed Giant!'

While Gumiloh was fetching his feather jacket, he attacked the enemy army. He killed everyone except the Seven-headed Giant and Bilantur.

Then he donned his coat of feathers. He sang to the Seven-headed Giant as he had sung to the Three-headed Giant. The giant answered as his predecessor had done. Thereupon Kichapi flew up to cut off the first of the giant's seven heads. Then he cut off the others, the giant talking as the other giant had done, until the last of his heads was gone. But the giant's body did not crash straight down. It swayed, first one way and then the other. Kichapi tried to fly away but the body swayed over him whichever way he turned. He could not escape. The giant's body came crashing down right on top of him.

"Ha! Kichapi is dead!" yelled Bilantur in triumph.

Kichapi's six brothers ran over to him. They pulled his body from beneath the headless corpse of the giant. Bilantur helped them to carry it over to the open space near the landing-place. In the middle of this open space they put the body down.

Gumiloh went over to Kichapi. She washed his body. Then she laid it out very carefully and decently, to make it look its best. The rest of the people sat around. They were all filled with sorrow except Bilantur. He was full of glee.

The people thought that Kichapi could never live again. But Gumiloh remembered the bottle of elixir which Kichapi had snatched from the Dragon-chief's mouth. She hurried to her house to get it. She poured the elixir over all parts of Kichapi's body. Bilantur stood by, watching.

Up leapt Kichapi. He grabbed Bilantur by the loin-cloth, and with a sweep of his knife, cut off his head.

The battle was over. The victory won. The people left the battle-field by the landing-place to reassemble on the longhouse verandah.

Kichapi is Reunited with his Family

Mats had been spread on the verandah. The heads were brought up. The people sat around them.

The brothers of Kichapi at last had a chance to question him. "How is it," they asked, "that you can be our brother? We had only one younger brother, and his name was Silanting Kuning."

"That is true," replied Kichapi, "but I am that brother who was called Silanting Kuning."

He told them how their mother had been pregnant with him for seven years and seven days. He told them that, after he had been born, he had gone shooting with the magical blowpipe born with him, and had not returned. He told them all this, because he knew that they would know it about Silanting Kuning, and it would prove that Silanting Kuning was he. When they heard his story, his brothers realized that he was truly their youngest brother. Kichapi then went on to tell them how the giants had given him his new name.

The work of skinning the heads and cleaning the flesh off them now began. All the men in the village shared in the task, except Kichapi, his six brothers and Kaleng.

That evening a marriage festival was held. Kichapi married Gumiloh and her sister Kumang Malidi. Each of Kichapi's brothers was given as a wife one of the girls who had been betrothed to Minyawai and his six brothers. This still left one of these girls. She was given to Kaleng in marriage.

The next morning Kichapi and his brothers, with Gumiloh and all the other wives, set off downstream for Kichapi's home. Kichapi wished very much to see his mother and father again.

When they reached the village, they waited at the landing-place while two of Kichapi's brothers, Mamang Marak and Mamang Marau, went ahead to the house of their parents. They greeted their mother and father, saying, "We met our youngest brother at the war."

"No. That cannot be," said Kichapi's mother. "He died many years ago, when he was a little boy."

"He is not dead," said the brothers. "He's alive! He's down at the landing-place now, in his boat with his wives."

"Then bring him up!" cried his mother. "Hurry! If he's there, bring him up!"

Kichapi's mother was now very excited. She hurried into her house to get a fine cloth, two arm-spreads long. She wished to stretch it down the step-way for her long-lost youngest son to hold as he came up.

Mamang Marak and Mamang Marau went back to the landing-place to tell Kichapi and the rest of the party that their parents were awaiting them. Kichapi, with the others, walked up to the longhouse. He mounted the steps, holding on to the fine cloth.

On the inner verandah, outside the home of Kichapi's mother and father, mats had been spread. Kichapi and his companions sat down upon them, had a smoke, and chewed betel. After they had sat awhile, they returned to the river to bathe. They came back to the verandah, and sat down to eat food which had been prepared for them.

When the meal was over, Kichapi's mother came to sit beside him. She questioned him eagerly, to find out if he were really her son. Kichapi told her of all his adventures, from the time of his being lost in the jungle until his marriage to Gumiloh.

Kichapi's mother now knew that he was really her long-lost youngest child, whom she had had to give up for dead. "Oh, yes! You are truly my son!" she exclaimed.

She was overjoyed. She embraced him. She kissed him. She kissed him, starting at his toes and kissing him all the way up his body until she reached his forehead.

His mother then called all the villagers to a meeting to arrange a festival to celebrate the recovery of her son. The festival was begun the following evening. It lasted three days. It was followed by a holiday of four days.[1]

The Festival for the Heads

On the morning of the fifth day after the end of the festival, when the holiday was over and people in the village could go to work in the fields again and persons who had been outside the village could now re-enter it, Kichapi and his party left to return to Gumiloh's village. They took Kichapi's mother and father with them.

Three days were spent on the journey. They arrived at Gumiloh's village in the evening of the third day.

In the village Pai Abang, Kaleng, Patu and Sangau Labung set about summoning all the people to a meeting.

When all the people had gathered together, Kichapi spoke, saying, "Tomorrow we must get everything ready for the festival for the heads of Minyawai, of the Three-headed Giant, of the Seven-headed Giant, of Bilantur, and of all the rest of the enemies we have slain."

The next day everyone stayed away from their ordinary work in the fields to prepare for the festival. The women cut bamboo, and divided it into sections, to make containers for cooking *pulit* rice. Some of the men gathered larger bamboo, and brought canoe-loads of it to the village, for making platforms for the offerings. Other men caught fish.

In the evening the festival began. It was due to last five days and nights.

On the first evening there was dancing and feasting. No offerings were made to the ancestors or demons because the food was not yet all cooked. Because no offerings had yet been made, the heads were not danced with on this night.

While the merry-making was going on, some of the men were busy preparing two sets of offerings,[2] which were placed one at each end of a platform built extending from the headhouse. Each set was made up of jars, plates, small bowls, and brass cannon, with two arm-spreads of white cloth wound round the whole. In the centre of one set were

[1] A *pantang*, or period of restriction, the main feature of which is cessation of work in the fields.

[2] In the local speech a set of offerings of this kind is known as a *sangar*.

placed seven long bamboo canes of the *buruh* species, with a spray of leaves left on top.[1] In the centre of the other set were placed five such canes. In each set there was a small platform on which food was to be placed later.

On the second evening, there were placed on the platforms in the sets of offerings cooked fowls, hard-boiled eggs, cooked *pulit* rice in its bamboo containers and cooked white rice wrapped as little parcels in leaves. On this night, too, the women who knew the prayers took the heads one after another, sat down, rested the heads on their knees, and prayed to them. The prayers they used are not known to the men. Then everyone, both men and women, danced with the heads. The old men who were skilled as priests sat before the sets of offerings and prayed to the ancestors, presenting the offerings to them as they did so.

Early on the morning of the third day pigs were slaughtered and singed. They were cut into pieces and cooked. Four pigs were killed for the offerings, two to be placed when cooked on the platform in each set of offerings. In addition, each household slaughtered a pig for its own use, either to eat or to give to others on the longhouse verandah to eat during the dancing and singing. In the evening the pigs intended as offerings were placed in the sets of offerings. The heads of the slain enemies were danced with throughout the night.

On the fourth night the festival was merrier than ever before. There was shouting and cheering as the men and the women danced, often with the heads. The dancing went on throughout the night until dawn.

On the fifth night, every man who had been a member of the war-party brought offerings of pork, fowl, rice cakes, preserved wild pig, preserved fish of large species such as *samah* or *karau*—small fish not being right for this occasion—eggs, cooked *pulit* rice in bamboo containers, a bowl of uncooked white rice, a bowl of uncooked *pulit* rice, and a bottle of wine. Their offerings were placed together on the inner verandah. These offerings were for the heads themselves. Old women who knew the right words prayed over them. Then the men danced, first with some of the offerings and then with some of the heads, until all the offerings and all the heads had been danced with. The women did not dance with either the offerings or the heads. Then there was ordinary dancing by both men and women, and shouting and cheering. When it was near dawn, the men took their

---

[1] Such a cane in the offerings is known as *burah bawar*.

offerings back to their own houses, where they and their families later ate them. The dancing and shouting and cheering were carried on until well after daylight. Gradually they died down as the people drifted off, tired, to sleep, and the festival came to an end.

After the festival there was a holiday from work in the fields, with all the usual restrictions to be observed at such times, for five nights. There was one unusual restriction, too—one which follows only the Festival for Heads. Men could not have intercourse with their wives for these five nights. They had to sleep on the inner verandah instead of in their household rooms.

When the five nights were over, and people were free again to do as they wished, Kichapi's mother and father returned home to their own village. Kichapi's six brothers and their wives went with them.

Kichapi decided to settle down with Gumiloh in her village. And together they lived in peace happily ever afterwards.

INDEX

Some other Oxford Paperbacks for readers interested in Central Asia, China, Japan, and South-East Asia, past and present

Cambodia

GEORGE COEDÈS
Angkor

MALCOLM MacDONALD
Angkor and the Khmers*

Central Asia

PETER FLEMING
Bayonets to Lhasa

ANDRÉ GUIBAUT
Tibetan Venture

LADY MACARTNEY
An English Lady in Chinese Turkestan

DIANA SHIPTON
The Antique Land

C. P. SKRINE AND
PAMELA NIGHTINGALE
Macartney at Kashgar*

ERIC TEICHMAN
Journey to Turkistan

ALBERT VON LE COQ
Buried Treasures of Chinese Turkestan

AITCHEN K. WU
Turkistan Tumult

China

All About Shanghai: A Standard Guide

L. C. ARLINGTON AND WILLIAM LEWISOHN
In Search of Old Peking

VICKI BAUM
Shanghai '37

ERNEST BRAMAH
Kai Lung's Golden Hours*

ERNEST BRAMAH
The Wallet of Kai Lung*

ANN BRIDGE
The Ginger Griffin

NIGEL CAMERON
The Chinese Smile

CHANG HSIN-HAI
The Fabulous Concubine*

CARL CROW
Handbook for China

PETER FLEMING
The Siege at Peking

ROBERT FORD
Captured in Tibet

MARY HOOKER
Behind the Scenes in Peking

NEALE HUNTER
Shanghai Journal*

GEORGE N. KATES
The Years that Were Fat

CORRINNE LAMB
The Chinese Festive Board

ALEKO LILIUS
I Sailed with Chinese Pirates

G. E. MORRISON
An Australian in China

DESMOND NEILL
Elegant Flower

PETER QUENNELL
A Superficial Journey through Tokyo and Peking

OSBERT SITWELL
Escape with Me! An Oriental Sketchbook

J. A. TURNER
Kwang Tung or Five Years in South China

JULES VERNE
The Tribulations of a Chinese Gentleman

Hong Kong and Macau

AUSTIN COATES
City of Broken Promises

AUSTIN COATES
A Macao Narrative

AUSTIN COATES
Macao and the British, 1637–1842

AUSTIN COATES
Myself a Mandarin

AUSTIN COATES
The Road

The Hong Kong Guide 1893

Indonesia

VICKI BAUM
A Tale from Bali*

'BENGAL CIVILIAN'
Rambles in Java and the Straits in 1852

VIOLET CLIFTON
Islands of Indonesia

MIGUEL COVARRUBIAS
Island of Bali*

AUGUSTA DE WIT
Java: Facts and Fancies

JACQUES DUMARÇAY
The Temples of Java

ANNA FORBES
Unbeaten Tracks in Islands of the Far East

HAROLD FORSTER
Flowering Lotus: A View of Java in the 1950s

GEOFFREY GORER
Bali and Angkor

JENNIFER LINDSAY
Javanese Gamelan

EDWIN M. LOEB
Sumatra: Its History and People

MOCHTAR LUBIS
Indonesia: Land under the Rainbow

MOCHTAR LUBIS
The Outlaw and Other Stories

MOCHTAR LUBIS
Twilight in Djakarta

MADELON H. LULOFS
Coolie

MADELON H. LULOFS
Rubber

COLIN McPHEE
A House in Bali*

H. W. PONDER
Java Pageant

H. W. PONDER
Javanese Panorama

JAN POORTENAAR
An Artist in Java and Other Islands of Indonesia

HICKMAN POWELL
The Last Paradise

F. M. SCHNITGER
Forgotten Kingdoms in Sumatra

E. R. SCIDMORE
Java, The Garden of the East

MICHAEL SMITHIES
Yogyakarta: Cultural Heart of Indonesia

LADISLAO SZÉKELY
Tropic Fever: The Adventures of a Planter in Sumatra

ALFRED RUSSEL WALLACE
The Malay Archipelago

HARRY WILCOX
Six Moons in Sulawesi

Japan

WILLIAM PLOMER
Sado

Malaysia

ODOARDO BECCARI
Wanderings in the Great Forests of Borneo

ISABELLA L. BIRD
The Golden Chersonese: Travels in Malaya in 1879

CARL BOCK
The Head-Hunters of Borneo

MARGARET BROOKE
THE RANEE OF SARAWAK
My Life in Sarawak

SYLVIA, LADY BROOKE
THE RANEE OF SARAWAK
Queen of the Head-hunters

F. W. BURBIDGE
The Gardens of the Sun

SIR HUGH CLIFFORD
Saleh: A Prince of Malaya

IVOR H. N. EVANS
Among Primitive Peoples in Borneo

HENRI FAUCONNIER
The Soul of Malaya

C. W. HARRISON
Illustrated Guide to the Federated Malay States (1923)

BARBARA HARRISSON
Orang-Utan

TOM HARRISSON
Borneo Jungle

TOM HARRISSON
World Within: A Borneo Story

CHARLES HOSE
Natural Man

W. SOMERSET MAUGHAM
Ah King and Other Stories*

W. SOMERSET MAUGHAM
The Casuarina Tree*

ROBERT PAYNE
The White Rajahs of Sarawak

Philippines

LEON WOLFF
Little Brown Brother

Singapore

RUSSELL GRENFELL
Main Fleet to Singapore

MASANOBU TSUJI
Singapore 1941–1942

C. W. WURTZBURG
Raffles of the Eastern Isles

Thailand

CARL BOCK
Temples and Elephants

ANNA LEONOWENS
The English Governess at the Siamese Court

SIBURAPHA
Behind the Painting and Other Stories

MALCOLM SMITH
A Physician at the Court of Siam

ERNEST YOUNG
The Kingdom of the Yellow Robe

* Titles marked with an asterisk have restricted rights.